D0422375

HOW TO STOP THE RUSSIANS

Without War

FRITZ STERNBERG

HOW TO STOP
THE RUSSIANS
Without War

NEW YORK

THE JOHN DAY COMPANY

Translated from the German by Ralph Manheim

Second Impression

CONTENTS

v

CHAPTER IV

EVEN A VICTORIOUS WAR WOULD BE NO SOLU-TION. AMERICA WOULD BE AN ISLAND IN A SEA OF BARBARISM

CHAPTER V

WE HAVE TO BE MORE PROGRESSIVE THAN THE RUSSIANS

HOW TO STOP THE RUSSIANS

Without War

CHAPTER ONE

THE WAR DANGER

THE WORLD today is in danger of war; to deny it would be not only unrealistic but foolhardy. For it is not by shutting our eyes to danger and taking refuge in the land of wishful dreams, but only by looking danger square in the face that we can hope to combat it.

True, the danger of war is present; but this does not mean that war is unavoidable. It can be avoided. With the help of a realistic, progressive American foreign policy, the present generation can hope to live in peace, even though undeniably the world situation today is far more menacing than after the First World War. The masses in all countries are pretty well aware of this. For them the First World War was a great turning point. By and large, the world had enjoyed a century of peace since the Napoleonic Wars; during this century from Waterloo to Sarajevo, hostilities, aside from the War of 1870, had occurred only on the periphery of the great industrial states.

1

After the First World War the peoples of the world believed that from then on there would be peace, and only with the Nazi seizure of power in Germany did they reluctantly begin to accustom themselves to the idea that there would be a new war.

The Second World War was not felt to be a turning point like the First World War; it was not regarded as the termination of an epoch. On the contrary. Today the whole war period is looked upon as just one stage in the unfolding of great historical events leading we know not whither.

And today, in sharp contrast to the years following the First World War, we are stricken with the fear of a new war, although the last one is scarcely over.

Only a short time after the military defeat of Germany and Japan, we are faced with the specter of a Third World War, and the question is no longer: Is it possible? but rather: Is it probable—or inevitable?

To speak of the possibility of a Third World War is to speak of a possible war between the United States and the Soviet Union; for only these two powers are capable of a conflict that would be a real world war.

The United States and the Soviet Union together are so strong that if they were allied, no coalition of countries could conceivably win a war against them for many years to come. They have emerged from the last war as the only real world powers. Yet these two powers are not equal in strength. Industrially and hence also from a military standpoint the United States is many times stronger than the Soviet Union; at the peak of war production the United States produced as much war material as England, Russia, and Germany together. On the other hand, the Soviet Union is the only power geographically situated on both the European *and* Asiatic continents; this geographical position offers an enormous political *and* military advantage.

The political situation of the world today is determined by the antagonisms between these two world powers, which stand at opposite poles in their economic and political systems.

The United States is the world's leading capitalist power; here more commodities are manufactured than in all the rest of the world together; economic power is concentrated in the hands of the great corporations. In the Soviet Union the state owns the means of production and private ownership of capital goods has been done away with.

The United States maintains the Anglo-Saxon system of political democracy, of personal and political freedom. Under the Soviet Union all personal and political freedom has ceased to exist, and the one-party state crushes any possible opposition with terror.

The two world powers are diametrically opposed in all their institutions.

But the differences in the economic and political

systems of the two countries do not by any means make war inevitable between them. In all epochs states with different economic and political systems have lived side by side. The divergent political systems of the United States and Russia have not led to war between them in the three decades from the October 1917 revolution to the present day. It follows that the conflicting systems do not adequately account for the tensions between the United States and Russia that have become so severe in the recent period.

And the danger to peace today does not reside primarily in the diametrically opposed economic and political views prevailing in the two world powers. For neither of the two has any idea of trying to impose its system on the other. The danger is not that the United States may attempt to impose its economic and political system on the Soviet Union by force of arms. Any idea of this sort is absurd; no one has ever expressed it, and there is no such trend. Likewise, there is no danger that the Russians may attempt to impose their system on the United States. This idea is equally absurd; it would be absolutely impossible to win over any serious percentage of the American population to totalitarianism in the Soviet style. It is highly significant that the American Communists have never elected a senator or congressman and that they have always been obliged to hide behind other names and front organizations.

4

In other words, the danger is not *inside* the two world powers; it does not consist primarily in any temptation on either part to attack the regime of the other country. No; the source of the danger is that in the course of the developments that culminated in the Second World War, the whole world outside of the United States and the Soviet Union, and especially the peoples of Europe and Asia, have been set in motion. *In Europe and Asia 1,500,000,000 people, almost three quarters of humanity, are on the march today*.

The circumstances of these 1,500,000,000 have undergone a fundamental change in the recent period. Tremendous dislocations have occurred. The direction in which these 1,500,000,000 people move will exert a profound effect on history, on the world parallelogram of forces, on the balance of power between the United States and the Soviet Union.

Today the Russians are in Berlin. Their policy is to draw all Germany into their sphere of influence. But Germany before the Second World War was the *second* largest industrial state in the world, with *one sixth* of world production.

The Russians today are on the Chinese borders; with their Communist allies, they dominate large areas of Manchuria and North China. Before the war Manchuria alone had an industrial production larger than that of all the rest of China, and in China alone lives more than one fifth of the world's population.

5

Germany alone is not strong enough to withstand a Russian Communist offensive. China alone is not strong enough to withstand a Russian Communist offensive.

As the greatest European and Asiatic power, as the only world power on the Eurasian continent, the Soviet Union has great opportunities for a gigantic expansionist offensive, the aim of which would be to change the world parallelogram of forces decisively in its favor, to diminish the gap that separates it from the United States as an industrial and military power.

The real danger lies in conflicting efforts to shape the future of the 1,500,000,000 in Europe and Asia, in a clash between the two world powers in their advance positions, whether in China or Korea, Greece or Iran, Germany, Italy, or France.

Recently it has become increasingly evident that this is the source of danger. But most attempts to analyze the situation have not gone very deep. Numerous articles in the press make it appear that the military and political collapse of Nazi Germany, the military collapse of Japan, the disintegration of the British Empire have produced a vacuum in the world, that the United States must fill this vacuum, and that if it does not, the Russians will do so.

This is one of those typical half-truths that are so dangerous just because they are half true but leave decisive factors out of account. We have not only an

6

economic and political vacuum in Europe and Asia; we have more; in reality we have in both continents one of the greatest processes of transformation that the world has ever seen.

The first thing we must know in order to analyze the *real* danger of a clash between the United States and the Soviet Union is: What is happening in Asia and in Europe?

CHAPTER TWO

WHAT IS HAPPENING IN ASIA AND IN EUROPE?

REVOLUTIONARY CHANGES have occurred in Asia as a result of the Second World War. The First World War had scarcely touched Asia; the Second World War, however, was in part an Asiatic war—in two respects: Asia was a battlefield and Asia was one of the stakes.

After its military defeat, Japan lost not only the territories conquered in the course of the Second World War, but also the conquests of the preceding decades. Aside from Russia, Japan had been the only highly industrialized power in Asia, the only country able to maintain and equip a modern army. It goes without saying that the Russians have been enormously strengthened in Asia by the complete disappearance of Japan as a military power. But the Second World War had other political consequences. Throughout Asia it gave new impetus to two great movements that had begun long before.

8

The first of these movements is the struggle of the Asiatic nations for independence and political freedom, the struggle against the old colonial imperialism. This struggle has already achieved great victories. England is leaving India; soon there will not be a single British soldier on Indian soil. India has ceased to be an object of British imperialism. It can and it wants to build its own economic and political future. The Indians themselves will decide whether or not to remain in the British Commonwealth. The fight for the liberation of India did not, of course, begin in the Second World War; it had been raging for many years. But the dislocation that the Second World War brought to England, Asia, the whole world, greatly speeded up the tempo of this struggle.

Today India is free, and the fact that it is free has had enormous repercussions throughout Asia. The struggles in the Dutch colonial empire have not been concluded; nor have those in French Indo-China. It is perfectly possible that Holland and France will again be victorious. But for how long? From the historical point of view, the era of old colonial imperialism is unquestionably drawing to an end. Now that Japan has been defeated and the British are leaving India, there is no doubt that all the nations of Asia will con-

9

tinue their march toward freedom and political independence.

THE STRUGGLE AGAINST FEUDALISM

Concurrently with their fight for political freedom, the people of Asia are carrying on another vast struggle. This is the struggle against the reactionary feudal landlords, for industrialization and higher living standards.

This movement is of critical importance for the conflict between Russia and the United States, and will be for many years to come.

The overwhelming majority of the Asiatic population lives by agriculture. Industrial production is extremely small. Immediately before the Second World War, British India, with a population of more than 350 millions, produced no more manufactured goods than Australia, with its population of 7 millions. The standard of living in all Asia is inconceivably low.

Colin Clark has attempted to compare the living standards of the various nations of the world. For this purpose he has reckoned the national income of the individual nations on the basis of what he calls an "International Unit," which he defines as follows: "An International Unit is . . . the amount of goods and services which could be purchased for one dollar in the United States on an average throughout the decade 1925–34." *

According to his calculations, the United States led the world before the Second World War with a total of 1,300 to 1,400 International Units per capita per year. Canada came next with 1,200 to 1,300 I.U.'s, and Great Britain third with 1,000 to 1,100 I.U.'s. On the other side of the picture were the people whose annual per capita income was below 200 I.U.'s, "the poverty line." Colin Clark assesses the total population of the world at 2,095 millions, and the combined population of the countries below the poverty line amounts to 1,113 million persons, or more than half of the total population of the world.

The overwhelming majority of these lived in the colonial and semicolonial areas of the world: 450 millions lived in China, 370.5 millions in British India, 65.42 millions in the Dutch East Indies, 117.8 millions in the rest of Asia (including French Indo-China, Korea, Formosa, Siam, Ceylon, and Malaya), and 106.09 millions in Africa (representing almost the whole of Africa with the exception of Egypt, Algeria, South Africa, Morocco, and Tunis).

The standard of living of the overwhelming majority of the population is so low that extreme poverty and starvation can be called the rule.

* Colin Clark, *The Conditions of Economic Progress*, London, 1940, pp. 2, 54, 57.

11

Conditions in British India are reflected in vital statistics: "The average length of life in India is low as compared with that in most of the western countries; according to the census of 1921, the average for males and females respectively was 24.8 and 24.7 years, or a general average of 24.75 years in India as compared with 55.6 years in England and Wales. It was found to have decreased further in 1931, being 23.2 and 22.8 years for males and females respectively." * Similar conditions prevail in all colonial countries of Asia, and in semicolonial countries such as China.

But today the peoples of Asia have awakened. They are no longer satisfied with political freedom but are now fighting for economic progress. The people of Japan, China, India, Korea, Manchuria, and the Dutch and French colonies are engaged in a struggle against the reactionary feudal landlords.

What has feudalism meant in Asia?

Much as the feudal regimes of Asia may vary in details, they are all alike in one point. The feudal lords own but do not cultivate the greater part of the land, while millions of peasants, in many regions the majority of the people, having no land, or insufficient land of their own, are compelled to work as tenants or share croppers for the feudal landlords.

* *Industrial Labour in India*, The International Labour Office, 1938, p. 8, based on the census of India in 1931, p. 98.

12

Agricultural methods are inconceivably backward.

The landlord's share commonly amounts to 50 per cent or more, although he himself does nothing. The result of this feudal exploitation is that agriculture is not modernized, that the great majority of the population lives in extreme poverty and hunger. It also hampers industrial development, since so impoverished a population can offer no expanding domestic market.

No economic progress is possible in Asia until this feudal organization of agriculture is eliminated or radically reformed.

EFFECTS OF THE JAPANESE DEFEAT AND THE LIBERATION OF BRITISH INDIA

Today this struggle is going on all over Asia—and the outcome of the war has greatly intensified it. Why? When Japan made its conquests in Korea, Manchuria, and China proper, it tried to find allies among the native population. And it found them everywhere, precisely among the old feudal landlords. They were willing to collaborate with Japan if their own economic interests were protected. And now the defeat of Japan has undermined the collaborationist landlord class in all the countries formerly occupied by the Japanese. The same is true of the European colonial empires. In order to cement their rule, the European imperialists had also sought allies; they too had found them

13

among the reactionary feudal classes, which for this reason they had consciously strengthened.

The British rulers of India have clearly understood this for over a century. Lord William Bentinck, governor general of India from 1828 to 1835, spoke very frankly of the alliance between British imperialism and the Indian feudal class. In an official speech during his term of office he declared: "If security were wanting against extensive popular tumult or revolution, I should say that the Permanent Land Settlement . . . has this great advantage at least, that it created a vast body of rich landed proprietors deeply interested in the continuance of the British Dominion and having complete command over the mass of the people." *

Because of the stagnation in economic development, the living standards of the majority of Indians remained at an extremely low level. The British therefore tried to improve matters by introducing certain agrarian reforms. However, the alliance of British imperialism with the Indian feudal classes seemed so necessary to them for the maintenance of their power and position that none of these reforms was permitted to touch the property basis of the feudal system that the British had helped to create. In a report of the Royal Commission on Agriculture in India, issued in

* Lord William Bentinck, speech made on November 8, 1829, reprinted in A. B. Keith's *Speeches and Documents on Indian Policy, 1750–1921,* Vol. I, p. 215.

1928, we read: "It will not be within the scope of the Commission's duties to make recommendations regarding the existing systems of land ownership and tenancy."

Now that the British are leaving India, the feudal landlords are losing their chief protectors.

To sum up: What is taking place in Asia? (1) The struggle of the Asiatic nations for freedom and independence; this struggle has already met with great success. And (2) a struggle for economic freedom against the reactionary landowning classes. The aims of this struggle are: radical land reforms, elimination or reduction of agricultural rents, modernization of agriculture. It is a struggle to provide the basis for large-scale industrialization and improved living standards for one half the human race.

This mighty movement is making itself felt throughout Asia today. American foreign policy must take it into account if any lasting success is to be achieved in Asia.

EUROPE'S STRUGGLE TO PRESERVE ITS DEMOCRACY AND INDEPENDENCE

Europe was once the industrial center of the world. At the time of the First World War it still produced more than the United States.

In consequence of the gigantic increase in Amer-

15

ican production during the Second World War and the devastation caused by the war in Europe, the United States today produces more than all Europe together.

But Europe is still of crucial importance to world development. In the coming years, which will decide the question of peace or war—and perhaps will decide whether or not the world is to descend into barbarism —Europe will be of far greater importance than Asia. The industrial production of the sixteen countries that under the Marshall Plan have turned to the United States for aid is far greater than that of the Soviet Union and its satellites, approximately twice as large as that of the Soviet Union alone—while the Soviet Union in turn produces far more industrial goods than all the nations of Asia together.

Like Asia, Europe has suffered profound dislocations; like Asia, it is searching for new roads. As in Asia, these dislocations did not, of course, begin with the Second World War.

The great industrial countries of Europe, like the United States, entered the First World War in a condition of social stability, following a period of industrial growth lasting many generations.

But in sharp contrast to the United States, they did not emerge from the First World War in a state of social stability. And the period *between* the two world wars was not a period of economic growth for Europe,

16

but a period of profound and continued dislocations. The inflation that gripped Europe after the First World War largely destroyed the holdings of the European middle class—particularly in Germany. In the mid-twenties, a certain stabilization occurred, but this prosperity was short-lived. The world economic crisis broke out. But in Europe it did not strike an economic and social structure with long years of prosperity behind it, or a population possessed of large savings, as in the United States, but a political and economic structure that had been shaken more severely than those of the United States by the First World War, and therefore was far more vulnerable after war and inflation.

The world economic crisis brought National Socialism to power in Germany; the National Socialists attempted to solve it by organizing a gigantic armaments production in the midst of peace.

For years before the outbreak of the Second World War in 1939, the people of Europe had been living in the expectation of it. Then the war broke out and Europe was again a battlefield; a Europe that had not fully recovered from the effects of the First World War was dealt a staggering blow by the Second World War.

The war was waged in the cities and industrial centers of Europe. And the widespread destruction it

17

caused has shaken the social structure of the Continent.

Europe is consequently faced with the necessity of achieving a new social and economic balance.

The urban middle class, which had already been so severely shaken by the inflation after the First World War, was now further impoverished and demoralized by the Nazi war economy and the Second World War. Today a new wave of inflation is passing over the whole of continental Europe. In these first postwar years, the middle classes are losing what they managed to preserve through the war.

There is no branch of European life, no section of the population that is not forced to undergo thoroughgoing changes.

In order to achieve an economic system similar to the American system of today, *Europe would have to return not to the period before the Second World War, but to the period before the First World War.*

The social and economic basis for a revival of the system of free enterprise has been destroyed by the upheavals of the last thirty years: the social basis, because a system of free enterprise requires a strong and flourishing middle class and the two world wars have left no such middle class in Europe; the economic basis, because Europe can solve its crises only by extensive *planning*, both in its home economy and in its trade relations with other continents.

Europe, which once possessed great colonial empires, must accept the fact (see also page 9) that the epoch of colonial imperialism is drawing to a close— and with it all the advantages that Europe once enjoyed in the old colonial territories.

Europe, which was once the center of world capital, with European capital invested in all continents, has grown poor in consequence of the two world wars. Its liabilities are greater than it assets. At a time when all of Asia is in the midst of a gigantic struggle for liberation, at a time when the colonial empires are fast being lost, an impoverished Europe must seek new roads by which to survive this epoch of change and upheaval *as an independent force*.

These new roads are not clearly laid out. Europe is still experimenting in many ways. But Americans should realize that Europe is not experimenting for love of experiment. It is not as if the war had left a viable form of European economy, which might perfectly well be continued, but was being endangered by experiments. Actually there is in Europe today no set and stable economic system such as we have in the United States. Instead there is an economic and social structure that has by no means recovered from the ravages of this war, and which must now adapt itself to a totally changed world situation.

Europe today is experimenting. It has not arrived at any final solutions.

But certain tendencies and trends can already be discerned, most clearly in England, in the attempts of the Labour government to reshape the social and economic life of its country by democratic socialist planning.

Democratic socialism means direct opposition to communism and the totalitarian state. Democratic socialism means, as the British Labour party has demonstrated ever since it came to power two and a half years ago, preserving political and personal freedom, parliamentary rule, the rights of minorities, and the right of opposition. Democratic socialism means freedom of the press and freedom of assembly; it means that in a few years' time the present government must answer to the British electorate.

The British Labour government therefore implies *no political break with the democratic history of England, but on the contrary demonstrates its continuity.*

However, the British Labour government took office with an *economic* program that had been discussed for months before by the voters throughout England. This program provided for drastic reforms, above all the socialization of basic industries such as coal and steel, transport, public utilities. If it is carried out, approximately 20 per cent of industry will have been socialized, while the remaining 80 per cent will still be in private hands.

It is noteworthy that this program for socializing basic industry was advocated not only by the British workers and the Labour government. In the whole period between the two world wars England never succeeded in solving its permanent unemployment problem, affecting millions of workers, and today it is in the midst of the gravest economic crisis in its history. Consequently increased government control of industry and the nationalization of certain industries were advocated by many groups outside the ranks of labor. The Conservative British opposition has declared—though indeed against an appreciable opposition in its own ranks—that if it is voted into the government at the next elections, it will retain a considerable share of the Labour government's nationalization measures.

England was not quite so severely shaken as the Continent by the two world wars, and consequently was able to preserve a certain stability and continuity in its institutions. The fight for the remolding of its social and economic life is being carried on without violence, by democratic socialist methods. One circumstance favoring this development is that so far the extremists of the right and left have found little support in England. The Communists, the most determined enemies of any democratic socialism, have never played a large role in England; in all these

21

years they have had no more than one or two representatives in Parliament. The reactionary semifascists have wielded no greater influence.

THE SITUATION ON THE EUROPEAN CONTINENT

The situation is different on the European continent.

In both world wars the Continent was a battlefield and suffered terrible devastation. In continental Europe there is no tradition of political continuity such as in England. Consequently the extremists are very much stronger. The Communist parties have a large and disciplined membership. Though they have never carried a clear majority in any country, they have become, particularly in France and Italy, the dominant force among the industrial working class. Throughout western Europe there are strong reactionary, more or less openly antidemocratic, fascist and semifascist groups. Even after the total military defeat, such groups exist in Germany.

The European continent can emerge from its present grave crisis only through the victory of those groups that are aiming to build up a new social and economic structure by democratic socialist planning. This new economic structure cannot be one exclusively of free enterprise. As in England, basic industry will have to be socialized.

22

The need for a *planned* transformation in all Europe, a transformation far beyond the scope of anything that free enterprise could accomplish under present circumstances, has become increasingly clear to many observers in the United States.

The sixteen nations that have applied for American aid under the Marshall Plan were instructed to draw up a program for pooling and developing their own resources. This is impossible under a system of free enterprise such as ours in the United States. In an editorial entitled "The Four-Year Plan," analyzing the Paris report of the sixteen nations, the *New York Herald Tribune* quite correctly writes: "There is for one thing the ironic, though secondary consideration that the United States, pursuing a policy dedicated to the revival of free international market and the abolition of all kinds of restrictive planning controls, should have found itself forced to instigate *one of the most remarkable attempts at international planning which our times have witnessed.* [Italics mine.] For this is a four-year plan, resembling in its production goals, consumption levels, allocations of resources, the celebrated Russian plans. . . ." *

Europe can survive only with the help of a *planned* economy.

But the crucial question (and crucial perhaps for the future not only of Europe) is whether this four-

* *New York Herald Tribune*, September 23, 1947.

year plan—in contrast to the Russian Five-Year Plans —will be carried on in accordance with *democratic* socialist principles and methods, such as the Labour government in England is observing in the execution of its own plan; whether, under this plan, personal and political freedom will be preserved.

This will be much more difficult on the Continent than in England, because the economic dislocation is far more severe, and because the progressive, democratic socialist forces are engaged in a bitter struggle with the right-wing extremists and the Communists.

The Communists are quite well aware that the democratic socialists are the most determined and most dangerous enemies of Communist expansion in Europe. They have recognized this fact and expressed it clearly in a proclamation of the nine Communist parties. The proclamation declares that there are two camps in the world today ". . . the camp of imperialist and anti-democratic forces, whose chief aim is an establishment of a world-wide American imperialists' hegemony and the crushing of democracy, and an anti-imperialist, democratic camp . . ." (This latter, of course, is the camp of the Communists themselves!) After an analysis of the tactical weapons at the disposal of the American camp, the proclamation resumes:

A separate place in this arsenal is reserved for the treasonable policy of the Rightist Socialists of the

24

kind of [Léon] Blum of France, [Prime Minister] Attlee and [Foreign Secretary] Bevin in Britain, [Socialist Leader Dr. Kurt] Schumacher in Germany, [President Dr. Karl] Renner and [Vice Premier Adolf] Schaerf in Austria, [Giuseppe] Saragat in Italy, and so on, who aim at hiding the true face of imperialism behind the mask of democracy and Socialist phraseology while in reality they serve as faithful toadies of the imperialists, bringing within the ranks of labor dissension and disruption and poisoning its conscience.

This clearly shows that any democratic socialist progress in Europe will meet with the sharpest resistance on the part of the Russians and their Communist puppets.

But resistance to democratic progress does not come from the Russians alone. Precisely because the situation in Europe today is so extremely grave, because the urban middle classes, which formerly served as a buffer between the extremist camps, have in many places almost been wiped out, precisely because all those groups that were directly or indirectly associated with National Socialism and fascism now fear for their vested interests, the democratic socialist forces are also faced with the most determined resistance from the right.

Such rightist reactionaries as the De Gaullists in France can for a time appear extremely strong. By banding with the Communists, they can have the majority of the electorate behind them, and in this way block any progress of a democratic socialist nature. It is even possible that—particularly because of the fear of the Communists that is now sweeping all Europe—they will come to power for a time. But in order to remain in power, they need foreign aid, for they have no program for solving the European crisis, for carrying the European nations through the present period of chaos. They have no program and they can have none, for a program capable of solving the European crisis must be above any narrow-minded nationalism, must be an *all-European* program.

On this point, the nationalists and reactionaries have nothing to offer. The Achilles' heel of the De Gaulle movement, for instance—and this is no accident—is that it has no program for solving the French or European economic and social crisis.

But the very fact that the reactionary nationalists have no program for solving the crisis and meeting the problems of a world in transformation is what makes the prospect of their taking power so dangerous. For if they were discredited, it is highly probable that the pendulum would swing in the other direction, that *the power would fall to the Communists*.

The European crisis can be solved only by those progressives who stand for responsible, parliamentary government, for political and personal freedom, and for a *planned* economy with nationalization of key industries. These are the democratic socialists and they represent the will of the European peoples. If the peoples of Europe were free to decide their future, without direct or indirect or threatened intervention from outside, there is little doubt that these progressive, democratic socialist forces would win out in the end, and that the future of western and central Europe would be entrusted to them.

Of course, they would also have great transitional difficulties to overcome; but the trend would be relatively clear.

In Asia the political trend is toward independence, sovereignty, freedom from colonial oppression, and the economic trend is toward elimination of feudalism, modernization of agriculture, increased industrialization, raising of the living standard, and elimination of poverty and hunger. In industrial Europe the political trend is toward personal freedom and democratic institutions, toward freedom of press and assembly; while the economic trend is toward a social democracy that will supply the foundations of these political freedoms, that will endeavor to solve the present European crisis through a plan that will put all of Europe's economic resources to the fullest use.

Europe today is not united; it consists of a number of states that were formed in earlier historical epochs. Its economic apparatus and its political mechanism as well are in many ways obsolete.

Europe will regain a decisive place in the present epoch of world powers only if it makes use of its present crisis in order to take an important step forward toward European unity; if, by a struggle against all reactionary, nationalistic, fascist, or semifascist forces, it can be reborn as a democratic socialist organism. This united Europe, to be sure, would never again be the center of the world that Europe once was, but it would represent a significant, independent force, powerful enough to play an important role in the present period. It would be a force capable of ensuring peace for a great many years to come.

But today Europe is by no means united in attacking its grave crisis, and consequently it is weak. The countries of western Europe are still sovereign states, but today they are exposed to pressure on all sides.

The course of European developments in the near future depends not only on internal trends but on the shape that the policy of the two world powers will assume in Asia and in Europe.

CHAPTER THREE

RUSSIAN AND AMERICAN POLICY IN ASIA AND EUROPE

WHAT ARE the aims of Russian policy in Asia?
Since the defeat of Japan, which automatically
ceased to be a great power, the Soviet Union has become *the only* great power on the Asiatic continent.
This has occurred at a time when all Asia, with its
population amounting to one half the human race, is
on the march.

RUSSIAN GOAL IN ASIA: NEW EXPANSION

The aim of Russian policy in Asia is unmistakable:
the enlargement of the Russian orbit.

Yet even if new Russian expansion is successful,
it does not necessarily follow that the territories
included in the Russian sphere of influence will be
formally incorporated in the Soviet Union. In Europe
the Russians rule all the countries between the Soviet
Union and Germany by means of puppet Communist

29

parties. They will attempt to do the same thing in Asia, for example in Korea, Manchuria, and certain Chinese provinces.

FACTORS FAVORING THE RUSSIANS IN ASIA

In order to achieve this aim, expansion in Asia, the Russians are very skillfully exploiting the social trends we have analyzed above.

Everywhere Russian policy supports the movements of the Asiatic peoples against feudalism and against colonial imperialism.

So far certain important factors have worked in favor of the Russians:

1. The Russians had no empire of their own in Asia; they have not obstructed industrialization in any of their own Asiatic provinces—on the contrary, they have pushed it to the utmost.

2. Through their October Revolution of thirty years ago, the Russians liquidated feudalism in their own country. Contradictory as their policy has been in other ways, they have always been perfectly consistent on one point: Wherever they have gone during and after the Second World War, to Korea or Poland, Manchuria or Hungary or the eastern provinces of Germany, everywhere they have carried out agrarian reforms, everywhere they have taken decisive steps toward the liquidation of feudalism. Today

their Communist allies are carrying out the same policy in China.

3. To European and American eyes the Russians are technically backward. Their per capita industrial production, their standard of living are far below those of central or western Europe, not to mention the United States.

All this is not true from the viewpoint of Asia. In comparison to the countries on the Asiatic continent, the Russians are representatives of technological progress; they have a far higher per capita production, and in comparison to most Asiatics, a higher standard of living.

4. Russia is governed by a terrorist dictatorship that suppresses all political and individual freedom. For any Russian expansion into the heart of Europe this is a great disadvantage—but not for an advance into Asia. In Asia the Russians will encounter hundreds of millions of people who have never experienced political and personal freedom in the American and western European sense; hundreds of millions of people who were the victims of European and Japanese imperialism, who were oppressed by this imperialism in league with their own feudal landlords, who have only one aim—to be a little less poor, a little less hungry—and who do not care whether it is a terrorist police state that helps them to achieve this goal.

To Asiatic eyes, as we have seen, the Russians appear as representatives of a higher living standard, a superior technology and industry. A further factor in their favor is that in the recent period the center of gravity of Russian industry has steadily shifted toward Asia.

As early as the first Five-Year Plans, the Russians, along with an increased industrialization of their European provinces, had begun to develop modern industries in the Asiatic provinces. This process became accelerated after the Nazi seizure of power in Germany, when German armaments production began to soar. The Russian reply to the German threat was not only to intensify their own armaments production, but to move important industries "behind the Urals," as far as possible from the German borders.

Then, during the war, when the German armies invaded Russia, numerous Russian factories were evacuated to Asia. At the same time those industries already situated in Asia were expanded, for Asiatic Russia was safe from the German armies and beyond bombing range.

With their present policy of *decentralizing* industry, calculated to minimize the effectiveness of a possible atomic war (see p. 91), the Russians are now

32

developing their Asiatic industries more rapidly than those situated in European Russia.

When the present Five-Year Plan is ended, the share of the Asiatic industries in Russia's total production will have changed as follows (the figures refer to the eastern share in the total Russian output):

	1940 per cent	1950 per cent
Iron Ore	29	44
Steel	34	51
Rolled steel	33	51
Coal	36	47.5
Oil	12	36

What is the consequence of this geographical shift of the Russian industries, of the strong emphasis on Asiatic development? The stronger the Russians are in their Asiatic provinces, the greater support they will have for expansion in that quarter.

UNITED STATES ATTITUDE TOWARD AGRARIAN REFORM IN ASIA

For a long time the danger of new Russian, or Communist, expansion in Asia was not fully recognized in American quarters.

Above all it was not recognized that the Russians, by supporting movements for agrarian revolution or

33

drastic reform, had put themselves in a position to win over millions of allies on their frontiers in Manchuria, Korea, and China. The *New York Herald Tribune*, in an editorial entitled "Communism and the Peasant," * has correctly stated:

Americans would understand better one of the assets of Russia if they were familiar with the life history of Stanislaw Zakrzewski. . . . Zakrzewski is a Polish peasant. As a result of land reform in his country he now owns twelve and a half acres. He and his wife still are so poor that they go barefooted except in the coldest weather. . . . But, despite their dire poverty, they are better off than they used to be. Before the war—before the Communists gained control of Poland—Zakrzewski was a day laborer for a landlord and received only about a dollar a week in hard money. Communists have done their utmost in countries along the Russian frontier to win the sympathy of men like Zakrzewski. In every land from Poland to Korea the Communists have been sponsors of land reform. They have tried to convince the peasants in many countries, from the Baltic to the Pacific, that the great conflict in the world today is between Communists, who divide vast estates and make it possible for the men who cultivate the land to own it, and a feudal system under which men work for a dollar a week. The Communists are aided in their endeavor by the fact that most of the people in the countries along the Russian frontier are not well equipped to understand the worst defects of Communism. They are not

* *New York Herald Tribune,* October 13, 1947.

34

prepared to distrust tyranny because *most of them never have enjoyed political freedom*. They may recognize that Communism means dictatorship—but it may seem to them a somewhat less disagreeable form of dictatorship than that with which they have been familiar in the past. Few Americans—even few of those in major government offices—understand this situation and, therefore, few of them understand the *strength the Russians have gained from sponsoring land reform in both Europe and Asia*. Americans are far too much inclined to believe that nobody, even a Polish peasant, can fail to recognize that Communism is evil and that the American system is far better. Americans usually ignore the fact that the Zakrzewskis of Poland and the Changs of China have had no chance to look at America but may have profited, at least a little, from Communist policies. Americans also are not conscious of how much success the Russians have had in distorting the truth to make it appear that the United States, because it is against Communism, is friendly to feudalism. Russian propaganda along this line already has had distressing results in some countries and will be a growing danger as long as Americans fail to realize that Europeans and Asiatics fail to see Communism from the same vantage point that Americans see it. [Italics mine.]

The liquidation of feudalism with complete agrarian reform is the crucial question in Asia today. It has enormous implications for Russian expansion. Only by taking this into account and acting accordingly can American foreign policy achieve any lasting success in Asia.

The United States won the Asiatic part of the Second World War almost singlehanded. The United States liberated China and the whole Asiatic continent from Japanese troops and Japanese pressure. Unlike the European industrial states, the United States has never had an empire in Asia. For the peoples of Asia it therefore had a clear anti-imperialist record. Moreover, it is industrially the leading world power, the only country that is in a position today to help the Asiatic nations with machines, raw materials, and capital, and to help speed up their development toward industrialization.

But all these advantages inherent in the American position will not suffice, if the United States does nothing about the question that is crucial for all Asia today, the question of agrarian reform and the elimination of the parasitic landlord class.

China—as well as Korea!—shows this clearly. The Communists are relatively strong in Manchuria and certain northern provinces of China; they are strong because the Russians turned over to them a large part of the armaments that they took from the Japanese. They are strong also because they have given land to the poor tenant farmers and peasants, and because millions of these poor tillers of the soil attach more importance today to agrarian reform in their own district than to the loss of certain liberties in the Chinese provinces controlled by the Communists.

The struggles between the Communists and Chiang Kai-shek's Kuomintang party began long before the Second World War. But *before* Japan made war on China, the Kuomintang had several factions. There was a relatively liberal wing, representing the urban middle classes, the intellectuals, the industrialists, the merchants, and a reactionary wing, dominated by the cliques of feudal landlords. In the war with Japan, China for a long time lost all its harbors and large cities. The government was moved to Chungking, in the interior of China. Since the merchants and industrialists had no field of operations in Chiang Kai-shek's territory, the Kuomintang came to be dominated more and more by the landlord cliques.

The Right Wingers [to quote an editorial in the *New York Herald Tribune*] cling to support of semi-feudal ideas in opposition to Communism, rather than to democratic ideas. They persist in the belief, no matter how often it is proved wrong, that Chinese armies recruited from peasant families will fight valiantly in support of inefficient and corrupt government of a semi-feudal character. This has been of such great advantage to the Reds that the Right Wingers should be on the Communist pay rolls. The Right Wingers have enabled the Communists to convince some Chinese that the conflict in China is not one between Communism and democracy but one between

37

Communism and feudalism. It is a conservative statement to say that the extreme Right Wing in China has been worth twenty-five divisions to Moscow.*

UNCONDITIONAL SUPPORT OF CHIANG KAI-SHEK BY THE UNITED STATES

Although these parasitic cliques of landlords dominate the Kuomintang today, our policy has been to give the Chinese government financial and military support, without insisting on thoroughgoing reform of Chinese agriculture as a condition of this support.

It is, however, absolutely impossible to combat the steadily increasing corruption in China as long as social conditions favoring it remain unchanged. Meanwhile, Chiang Kai-shek's policies are determined by a parasitic class that has built up enormous fortunes through the almost uncompensated labor of millions of tenants living in unspeakable poverty.

As long as these conditions prevail, the struggle against the Communists in China will be hopeless.

With certain differences, the situation in Korea is similiar to that of China. The country is divided into two occupation zones: Russian in the north, American in the south. In the north the Russians have put through extensive land reforms and given land to the poor tenants and agricultural laborers. In this way

* *New York Herald Tribune*, August 31, 1947.

they have attempted to win popular support for the puppet government they have set up.

The Americans have provided no adequate reply to this Russian policy, which attempts to turn the desire of the Korean people for land reform into a force for Russian expansion.

The *Herald Tribune* writes: "The United States, unfortunately, never has had a program for Korea that went much farther than opposition to Communism. This is not enough in Korea, nor anywhere else. . . . Land reform was postponed until it could be carried out at some time in the future by the Korean government. It seemed difficult, under American political theories, to do anything else—although vast areas of land had been controlled for years by the Japanese or by Korean puppets of the Japanese." *

This policy of postponement on our part cannot fail to alienate the sympathies of the Asiatic masses, who know that in territories under the Russian control these questions are not being "postponed." It alienates not only the millions of impoverished peasants, but also many middle-class liberals and intellectuals who are convinced that agrarian reform is the prerequisite for any real progress.

* *New York Herald Tribune*, October 1, 1947.

There is an additional factor that is beginning to
arouse distrust toward us in those groups that oppose
communism as well as reaction: our policy toward
Japan.

Japan was the enemy of China. Every Chinese
knows the frightful devastation created by the Japanese in China. Not individual groups, but almost the
whole of the Chinese people suffered from Japanese
imperialism and militarism. They are therefore bit-
terly opposed to any policy that might make possible
a new Japanese imperialism and militarism. They
were solidly for the United States as long as American
policy was unmistakably opposed to any possible re-
surgence of Japanese militarism. But today the Chinese have become doubtful on this point; they are
afraid that, if antagonism between Russia and the
United States should become more acute in Asia and
elsewhere, certain American groups would favor a
strong Japan as a springboard for operations against
the Soviet Union and even as a possible ally.

"The Japanese peace settlement," writes Tillman
Durdin in the *New York Times*, "offers the most dis-
turbing prospects that China will not be able to co-
operate with the United States. The Chinese fear the
Americans will favor a much higher economic level

40

for Japan and much less post-treaty military and political supervision than China desires." * With this Japanese policy, we are losing still more sympathy in China.

DANGER OF SUPPORTING REACTION IN ASIA

So far our policy has essentially consisted in trying to stop Communist expansion in China through military and financial support of the Chiang Kai-shek government, *although this support meant working against the agrarian reforms that are absolutely indispensable to China.*

The danger of such a policy is already becoming increasingly evident. Although we may temporarily keep the Chiang Kai-shek regime with its reactionary landlord cliques in power and thwart Communist expansion in this way, in the long run we shall not be creating a healthy social basis for the government we are supporting. By maintaining a feudalistic regime in power through our support, we are alienating countless millions of Chinese and driving them into the camp of the Communists—that is, the Russians. And not, as might be supposed, because they are Communists—most Chinese peasants, like peasants all over the world, are anticommunist—but because they

* Tillman Durdin, "Chinese Consider Shift to Moscow," *New York Times,* September 28, 1947.

would rather see an agrarian reform that would give them land than the preservation of feudalism through American support.

The United States went to war against Japan because it refused to recognize Japan's dominant role in China. Today Japan has lost out in China and China is faced by a new danger. It is in danger of becoming a satellite of the Soviet Union, not only because of Russian military strength—Japan had that too—but because the Russians have known how to use the mighty currents that are transforming all China today for their own expansionist ends.

Up until now we have failed to meet the Russian challenge in one decisive point. By military means *alone* it is not possible to stop Russian expansion in Asia. Moreover, if our only answer is military and financial support of a corrupt government based on reactionary landlords, if we do not exact drastic social and agrarian reforms, the war danger in Asia will merely be increased.

THE RUSSIAN POLICY IN EUROPE

What is the goal of the Russians in Europe? What is the meaning of Europe for Russian expansion, for the world balance of power, for the relations between the United States and the Soviet Union?

Before the outbreak of the Second World War the
Soviet Union had approximately 12 per cent or one
eighth of the world's industrial production. At that
time the United States had just 40 per cent of world
production. Before the Second World War, in other
words, the production of the United States was approximately three times that of the Soviet Union.

The Second World War brought a considerable
shift in favor of the United States. American production and productive capacity increased enormously.
During the war we produced, and we still produce today, at least 50 per cent more goods than before the
war. This fact alone would make our production
approximately four and one-half times that of the
Soviet Union.

But Russian production dropped during the war.
For years Russia was a battlefield; the scorched-earth
policy of the Russians at the time of their first defeats
by the Germans, and later the systematic destruction
practiced by the retreating German armies, cut down
production and greatly decreased productive *capacity*.
Today the Russians are busy repairing their war losses
and getting back to their peacetime level. But even if
they succeed in this, the United States will retain the
enormous superiority of four and one half to one over
the Soviet Union.

The Soviet Union will therefore not be able in the foreseeable future to overtake the United States as an industrial or, it follows, a military power.

The Soviet Union can reduce this lag behind the United States, but by its own resources it cannot hope to bridge the gap entirely. This is clearly shown by Stalin's much-quoted speech, delivered on February 9, 1946, at the time of the first postwar election. In this speech Stalin gave a few figures regarding the production levels that the Russians hoped to achieve after another three or four Five-Year Plans, that is, in fifteen to twenty years, and compared these statistics with certain figures relating to the past.

During the period between the two world wars, Russian industrial output was expanded tremendously as a result of the Five-Year Plans. In his speech Stalin gave the following figures for 1940, the year preceding Germany's invasion.

The Russian production amounted to:

18,300,000 tons of steel,
15,000,000 tons of pig iron,
166,000,000 tons of coal.

In the same year German steel production was approximately 25,000,000, pig iron 18,500,000, coal 190,000,000.

The relation between German and Russian production had undergone a decisive change. German production compared to Russian production was no longer four or five times as large as in the period of the First World War; the ratio was now only five to four.

Russia's production had grown to be as large as that of all Europe without Germany and England. German per capita production was no longer ten times greater than that of the Soviet Union, but only three to four times greater.

THE SOVIET UNION ALONE IS STILL FAR BEHIND THE UNITED STATES

And what is Stalin's picture of the future?

The trend is clearly shown by a comparison of Stalin's figures for Russian production goals with figures showing the industrial production of all Europe before the Second World War.

	steel	pig iron	coal
Russian figures according to Stalin's speech	60,000,000	50,000,000	500,000,000
Total Europe without Russia	52,000,000	40,816,000	571,157,000

The goal that the Russians have set themselves is made perfectly clear by these figures. This goal is a *Russian production equal to that of all the rest of Europe, including Great Britain and Germany, before the Second World War.* (A certain lag in Russian

45

coal production is more than compensated by the fact that Russian oil production is many times that of the rest of Europe.)

By the outbreak of the Second World War Russia had far surpassed English as well as French production and had become, after the United States and Germany, the world's third industrial state. In per capita production, however, it still remained far behind western Europe and Germany. The present Russian goal is to raise per capita production to the German, or western European, level.

For the sake of our analysis let us assume that the Russians are 100 per cent successful in these future Five-Year Plans. *Even then they will remain far behind the United States.*

In 1965–70 the Russians, with 60,000,000 tons of steel, would still be producing only two thirds as much steel as we already produced at the time of the Second World War. Moreover, the United States can greatly increase its production and productive capacity in the same interval.

THE SOVIET UNION NEEDS LARGE NEW CONQUESTS IN ORDER TO CATCH UP WITH THE UNITED STATES

Since the defeat of Germany the Soviet Union has become the second industrial world power, but for the present and the near future, it cannot hope to equal,

46

or even approach, the first world power, the United States.

But this is true only if the Soviet Union *alone* is considered.

This brings us to the most pressing motive of Russian policy in Europe: The Russians *alone* cannot hope to equal the United States. But if the Russians can draw the leading countries of Europe into their orbit, they can become as strong as the United States.

In the period before the Second World War, when the Soviet Union had approximately one eighth of world production, Germany had approximately one sixth. Though the Soviet Union *alone* cannot equal the United States, it can hope to do so by drawing Germany and the countries between Germany and Russia into its orbit.

For this reason Europe is the key to the world balance of power. If the Russians gain control of the whole European continent, they may not only reduce the gap between themselves and the United States, but actually *equal the United States*.

Russian expansion in Asia may be of crucial importance in the more distant future. But even if the Russians make great advances in Asia, Asiatic production is so small that *for the present* this will do little to diminish Russia's industrial and military lag behind the United States.

But success in Europe would be a different story.

Europe was once the industrial center of the world; this is no longer true, but it is still strong enough to have a decisive effect on the world balance of power. The central goal of Russian policy in Europe now becomes clear: to gain control of the European economy by expansion, or else to weaken and paralyze it.

THE THREE WEAPONS OF RUSSIAN EXPANSION IN EUROPE

Russia has three main weapons with which to implement its policy of expansion in Europe: (1) the Red armies; (2) the Communist parties; (3) the European crisis.

The Red armies not only defeated the German armies on Russian soil, but drove them across the border as far as Berlin. Today the Red Army is in Berlin. In the final phase of the Second World War, Russia demonstrated its military strength to all the countries and peoples lying between the Soviet Union and Germany. Today the Red Army, whether it is still in these countries or has already left them, dominates them all in actual fact.

All the countries that lie between the Soviet Union and Germany are more or less within the Russian sphere of influence. These include Poland, Hungary, Czechoslovakia, and the Balkans (with the exception of Greece), i.e., Bulgaria, Rumania, and Yugoslavia.

48

Apart from territorial gains as a result of the recent war, therefore, the Soviet Union influences an area in Europe in which before the war over 90,000,000 people lived.

These countries are at very different stages of industrial development. Czechoslovakia, for instance, was on about the same industrial level as the highly developed countries of continental Europe, while the Balkan countries were industrially very backward. The production of those German territories now incorporated into Poland must be considered and these include Upper Silesia, which was very highly developed industrially. In 1929 the industrial production of the countries between the Soviet Union and Germany amounted to almost as much as Russia's own, and as a result of the war the Soviet Union now largely controls industrial production in these countries.

Today the Red Army is occupying the eastern zone in Germany; in this zone the Russian terror has suppressed the party of the democratic socialists. Here the Russians have created a "Party of Socialist Unity," which is nothing other than a Communist party; and the leaders of this Party of Socialist Unity rule eastern Germany as Russian puppets.

The Russian zone of Germany is not so strongly industrialized as western Germany; it is, however, far more intensively industrialized than any of eastern

Europe. Before the war it had roughly 25 per cent of German production, or roughly 4 per cent of world production.

When the Russians reach their own peacetime level, they will control 12 per cent of world production in Russia proper, plus 4 per cent in the countries between Russia and Germany and 4 per cent in Germany. When reconstruction outside of Russia has also been completed, the Russians will therefore control roughly 20 per cent of world production.

By their expansion in Europe, the Russians have already achieved a very considerable increase in their industrial and military production, but up until now, *this has not been sufficient to make a decisive difference in the world balance of power.*

THE COMMUNIST PARTIES IN EUROPE

An increase sufficient to do this would require an advance into western Europe: France, western Germany, Italy, England. So far the Red Army has not penetrated into these countries. Here the Russians are primarily making use of their second weapon: the Communist parties.

The most recent proclamation of the nine Communist parties has completely punctured the fiction that the individual Communist parties were in any way independent. This proclamation has made it perfectly clear that the Russians determine the policy of all the Communist parties, such as the Communist party of France and the Communist party of Italy.

The immediate future of the world will be decided in western Europe. Here lies the world balance of power. The nations of western Europe produce more coal and steel than the 300,000,000 people of Russia and its satellite states.

This, therefore, is the critical point at which to stop the Russians.

The Russians have strong Communist parties on the European continent; they are particularly strong in France and Italy, where they have won over the majority of the industrial workers; so far they are not so strong in western Germany, where the overwhelming majority of the workers are with the democratic socialists and a part of them are in the Catholic parties.

Western Europe presents far greater obstacles than Asia to Russian expansion. Russia is industrially backward in comparison with western Europe and Germany. With a population less than half as large as Russia's, Germany produced more than Russia before the Second World War. Western Europe has roughly three times the per capita production of the Soviet Union. Hence the Russians do not appear as representatives of industrial or technical progress; in western European eyes they are an industrially backward people.

The living standard of Germany and all western Europe is very much higher than that of the Russians. It is so much higher that the Russian authorities had great difficulty with the returned Red Army men who had seen with their own eyes how much better the German workers lived than the average Russian worker.

Another obstacle to Russian expansion in Europe is presented by Europe's libertarian traditions. In western Europe feudalism was pretty well done away with a long time ago. Western Europe passed through the French Revolution; western Europe knows the meaning of political and personal freedom. In Germany, it is true, political and personal freedom were destroyed by the Nazis, but that does not mean that the Germans now yearn for a new tyranny. They have no desire to exchange the Nazi totalitarian state for a Russian totalitarian state.

It is no accident that the Communist parties in western Germany are far weaker than those of France and Italy. In spite of the iron curtain, communications of all sorts exist between the Russian-occupied zone of Germany and the western zones. The Germans in the west know with what terror the Russians rule their zone, and hundreds of thousands of refugees from the Russian zone are the living evidence of this terror.

If in spite of these factors the Russians are to expand beyond the zones now held by the Red Army, it cannot be done through the Communist parties alone. They require the support of a third weapon.

THE EUROPEAN CRISIS

In a prosperous Europe the Russians would have no prospects. But Europe is not prosperous today, and years will be needed to restore even a semblance of stability and to remedy the food situation. The report of the sixteen nations that have turned to the United States for aid states: "Even in four years' time the consumption of goods in Europe will still be significantly below pre-war, even assuming full success of the agricultural programs. The hard fact of this report is that there is not enough food in the world to give Europe as much as it had pre-war, and *that even in 1951 supplies will still be very short.*" [Italics mine.]

Europe has too little food for its population and will not produce enough in the next few years. Europe is lacking in numerous raw materials; Europe is impoverished.

Consequently Europe will need years to adapt itself to changed world conditions. These years of crisis, these years of want, these years of economic and social upheaval are the danger period for Europe.

The European crisis is a golden opportunity for the Russians; for the Russian state, precisely because it is a dictatorship, can always throw its economic

53

surplus, small as it may be, in the spot where it will do the most good politically.

In 1947, for example, France had the poorest harvest in many years. The Russians in this same year had their best harvest. At a time when France was menaced by starvation if it did not receive foreign aid, Russia had millions of tons of grain available for export. And this winter will not see the end of the European crisis. It will continue for years despite temporary letups.

If the crisis is solved in a *progressive* way, the prospects for the Russians are small. Then the overwhelming majority of the population in western Europe and western Germany will oppose any Russian expansion.

But is it certain that the crisis will be solved in a progressive way? Is there not a possibility that (1) aid will be inadequate and the crisis will last longer than necessary, and that (2) reactionary solutions will first be attempted?

This is one of the decisive points in our analysis and in the history of our time. For here the question arises: What is the United States doing in Europe at this time of European crisis and social transformation?

Some time was required before the full gravity of the European crisis was understood in the United States.

It was obvious, of course, that a shortage of the most necessary commodities was inevitable immediately after the Second World War. But by 1946, when the countries of western Europe—with the exception of Germany, of course—had taken long strides toward recovery, the chief trouble seemed to be over. It took the threat of starvation in the winter of 1947–48 to make the American public realize that the recovery in 1946 had been purely temporary; that Europe is not in a period of cyclic slumps and minor economic disturbances, but is undergoing gigantic transformations, *fraught with the gravest political dangers.*

It required the deterioration of relations between the United States and Russia to convince large numbers of Americans that the crucial question is not whether the Marshall Plan is a good investment from the purely economic point of view. The question of American aid, which will help to determine the future of Europe, is primarily a political one. This aid can help to forge a weapon that may well stop Russian expansion, perhaps at the most crucial point. Large numbers of Americans have realized that the expenditure involved in aid to Europe, although considerable, is to our own interest. For the cost of this aid is only a fraction of what the United States would have to spend if the Russians were to expand any farther in Europe.

Although the majority of the American people now supports aid to Europe, there is still a strong opposition. Hence there is a constant danger that our aid will be too little to carry through the enormous transformations that are needed, and that it may for some countries come too late, particularly since it will certainly take Europe years to achieve any real economic stability.

DANGERS OF A REACTIONARY DEVELOPMENT IN EUROPE

But even if we are optimistic and assume that isolationism will be defeated in this point, that Europe, if only at the eleventh hour, will obtain not too much, but at least the most essential aid, the danger still remains that American aid may be granted subject to conditions that play into the hands of the European reactionaries, creating a social situation that will help the Communists and Russians to shattering successes.

For a time perhaps we can stop the Russians in Asia by supporting the Chiang Kai-sheks and the landlords, but during this time many millions of Asiatics will be driven into the Communist camp, since in the meantime conditions favorable to the Communists will have been created. A similar development is possible in Europe. It is therefore necessary, not only that sufficient aid should be given on time, but also that the aid should not be given subject to conditions that would obstruct Europe's great historical trend toward a democratic socialist transformation of its society, subject to conditions that would help the reactionaries. For today that would mean, after a brief interval, the Communists.

Our aid should stop the Russians. But it should stop them not only in 1948, but permanently. It can do this only if the conditions under which it is given are compatible with the aims and desires of the majority of Europeans, with their plans for molding their future and rebuilding their social and economic life.

It must be said that up until now our aid has not met with these requirements. We have already taken steps directed against this trend in Europe; and there is great danger that we may continue on this catastrophic road.

AMERICAN POLICY IN GERMANY

The European crisis has been intensified by the artificial holding down of production in western Germany.

57

A crucial point in any program for European reconstruction is therefore the speeding up of production in western Germany, and particularly the Ruhr. The Ruhr was the industrial heart of Germany and one of the most important centers of European production. Its steel output was greater than that of England, its coal output greater than that of France. Even before Hitler came to power, the Ruhr industrialists, who had never been democratically minded, supported the Nazis. From 1933 to 1939 they helped the Nazis to build their war machine. They collaborated with the Nazis up to the last moment.

The Ruhr is situated in the British zone. The Labour government did not return the Ruhr coal mines to their private owners, but nationalized them. This nationalization of the coal mines was one point in a larger British program.

On October 22, 1946, British Foreign Minister Bevin declared in an important speech before the House of Commons that England had assumed control of coal and steel production in the Ruhr; that the machinery and chemical industries would be taken over next; and that these industries would never again pass into private ownership. Mr. Bevin correctly pointed out that the Ruhr industrialists were the allies of Nazism and militarism and should pay for it.

I repeat: The plan of the British Labour government provided for socialization of basic industry in the Ruhr, the industrial heart of Germany. The British intended to synchronize their own socialization program with their program for Germany and in this way create a basis for a progressive development in all western Europe.

They acted in accordance with the will of the Ruhr population. The German coal miners, in particular, had many times voted by large majorities for socialization of the mines.

But in the fall of 1947 the crisis in England became so severe that the British had difficulty in meeting 50 per cent of the occupation costs for the combined western zone, and in providing food supplies for their own zone in Germany.

They turned to the United States for help. And in the negotiations the United States insisted that no step toward socialization should be undertaken in the Ruhr.

"During the conference, Mr. Thorp [Assistant Secretary of State for Economic Affairs] put the United States on record as flatly opposed to the British plan for socialization of the Ruhr mines and industries. . . . It was understood at the outset of the negotiations that British Foreign Secretary Bevin had agreed with Secretary Marshall that the question of socialization in the combined zone was to remain 'on ice' for from three to five years." *

* *New York Times*, September 11, 1947.

59

For the present the British accepted this "postponement," though with a heavy heart, for they know what is at stake. They accepted it because they are in such urgent need of American help.

Up until now, the question of the future development of western Germany has been "postponed." So far it has only been decided that no step is to be taken toward socialization, that is to say, toward democratic socialist transformation.

It can be taken for certain that the British Labour government will resume the struggle for this decisive point when the time seems ripe.

But already the American policy that annulled the first steps toward democratic socialist transformation has called forth grave consequences.

1. This American policy of restoring the old German industrial management, with its large percentage of Nazi collaborators, can be carried out only against the will, and consequently over the latent opposition, of the German workers. It is plain that a continuance of this policy can benefit only the Communists, who are able to point out that the most reactionary groups are favored by the United States.

2. It is a difficult matter in itself to overcome *French* opposition to any considerable revival of German industry. The French experience of German aggression is still too fresh. But if this rebuilding of German industry is not based on progressive, demo-

cratic socialist forces, but is directed by those groups that helped Hitler to organize the war and have always co-operated fully with German militarism, there is no doubt that French opposition will increase many times over.

3. In consequence of the gravity of the present British crisis, it has become clear to the British that they must abandon their *insular* attitude, that the progressive development of England is inextricably bound up with that of the European continent. Only in collaboration with the Continent will it be possible to build an economic body that will be strong enough economically and politically to maintain its independence in the present epoch of *world* powers.

There will be grave danger for the development of a prosperous Europe if one of its most essential factors, the reconstruction of German industry, assumes forms that the British government does not approve and accepts only because, in the present acute British crisis, it is in no position to resist.

Opposition to the American policy in Germany, and particularly in the Ruhr, is not limited to the British Labour party, but extends to all groups that fear Russian expansion in Europe. When the American plans for the Ruhr became known, the influential British weekly *The Economist*—which in many points opposes the Labour government—wrote, in an article entitled "The Shadow of the Ruhr": ". . . An American plan to base European revival upon a German heavy industry built up as a cartel by private capital might well bring the Communist Party to power in France and in the Ruhr." *

So far British protests have not succeeded in changing our German policy on this point. Every step toward the socialization of basic industry in Germany has been stopped. The consequences for Germany are that all the reactionary groups that collaborated with Hitler before and during the war feel strengthened, since it is actually they whom the American policy supports, and that the Communists, who are most outspoken in denouncing this policy, gain followers among the German workers, because their determined foes in the German labor movement, the democratic socialists, are of course weakened by this American policy.

If the Communists become as strong in western Germany as, for example, in France, there is no doubt that the situation will be extremely precarious, with the Red Army already in eastern Germany.

AMERICAN POLICY IN WESTERN EUROPE

There is no government of the German people in Germany. Consequently the American policy, which blocks democratic socialist progress, which supports

* *The Economist,* July 12, 1947, p. 52.

the old vested interests, can be carried out *administratively as part of the occupation policy*.

In the countries of western Europe, the countries that have applied to the United States for aid under the Marshall Plan, this cannot be done so simply. They are sovereign states, they have their own governments. We can't simply say to them: You will get American aid only if you give up your plans for reshaping your social and economic structure along socialist lines.

But Mr. Stassen, a possible Republican candidate for the presidency, has done just that. In one of his speeches, he has declared:

"We should expect agreements that the governments with which we work will not move farther away from individual economic freedom and will not go down the sad trail of increasing nationalization or socialization or government-ownership, which would result in lower production for them and would negate the constructive efforts we are making, and would make more difficult our own free economic future."

Mr. Stassen, of course, spoke only as a private person, not as a representative of the American government. So far there are no *official* American statements demanding the abandonment of plans for a democratic socialist transformation as a condition for American aid to Europe—which, in effect, would amount to *open* United States interference in the in-

63

ternal affairs of the western European countries, and *open* support of European reactionaries and semi-fascists.

There are no official statements. That, after all, would be too clumsy. Any such official formulation of the American policy might produce results exactly the opposite of those desired; it might well arouse overwhelming European opposition going far beyond the ranks of labor and the progressives. For such a policy could be construed only as an attack on the sovereignty of the European states in one of the most important, if not *the* most important, point for their future.

Consequently American diplomacy has proceeded with caution thus far. Its methods are indirect. The *Report of the Harriman Committee* declares expressly: "While this committee firmly believes that the American system of free enterprise is the best method for obtaining high productivity, it does not believe that any foreign-aid program should be used as a means of requiring other countries to adopt it. The imposition of any such conditions would constitute an unwarranted interference with the internal affairs of friendly nations."

But such American declarations are not enough, if they are contradicted by American *actions* in the heart of Europe, the Ruhr; if our aid to Europe is to be administered predominantly by express opponents of all socialism; and if such declarations are looked upon as mere phrases here at home.

Mr. Arthur Krock, head of the Washington bureau of the *New York Times*, writes:

And though it uses different words, the Harriman committee recommends, as Harold E. Stassen does, that continued credits be conditioned on performance . . . it . . . also says that "continued assistance" should depend on whether the "participating countries take all practicable steps" to attain the goals they have set for themselves. *It isn't likely that the Harriman committee and Mr. Stassen would disagree privately on his proposition that further socializing of British industry is not one of these "practicable steps."* * [Italics mine.]

That seems clear enough.

By its policy in the Ruhr the United States has clearly shown that it is *against* any progress in the democratic socialist sense, when it has the power to decide *alone*. It has shown what roads it would prefer for Europe if it could decide directly. This is now known to the three significant groupings in the European countries; it is known to the reactionaries in Germany, France, Italy, and England as well; it is known to the democratic socialists; it is known to the Communists.

Every reactionary group knows that in its struggle

* *New York Times*, November 11, 1947.

against democratic socialism, in its efforts to sabotage progressive developments, it can count on direct or indirect American support. All democratic socialists know that they must reckon not only with the opposition of the reactionaries and semifascists at home, but also with probable American support to the reactionaries.

And the Communists, of course, will attempt to profit by these contradictions in every possible way. They will say to the workers, who in Europe, unlike Asia, make up roughly half of the population: "The democratic socialists have never been able to get you anywhere. They will fail again. They are not being supported by the Americans, and without American support they cannot succeed. You workers must choose between a comeback of the reactionaries, nearly all of whom were in league with the Nazis, and us. And behind us stands a world power, the Soviet Union."

Direct or indirect American support of the reactionaries is a crushing blow to the democratic, progressive socialists in Europe.

Perhaps certain people in the United States will answer: Very well, then these democratic socialists will lose their influence. We have no more interest in them than in our own socialists in America. We are interested in building up a system of free enterprise in Europe, even if it is strongly reactionary.

The answer to this is: In Europe, which went through two world wars, through inflation and world economic crisis and years of National Socialist tyranny; in Europe, where the urban middle classes have been all but wiped out, an American form of free enterprise is not possible. Any attempt to create such a system artificially is doomed to failure.

No form of capitalism is possible in Europe today except through American support of European reaction; it is possible only in fascist or semifascist forms. It is no accident that in the present French crisis, the militarists, the reactionaries, the semifascists, the representatives of the vested interests have gathered together in De Gaulle's camp, just as fifteen years ago the German militarists, nationalists, reactionaries, the Ruhr industrialists gathered together in the camp of National Socialism, of Hitler.

Hitler's National Socialism could not endure; it was shattered by the war. That should be a warning.

This reactionary, fascist, or semifascist capitalism cannot last in Europe, any more than the rule of the reactionary landlord cliques in Asia can last, since the compelling historical trend is against them.

Here the objection may be raised: Perhaps this is true, perhaps an American system of free enterprise is no longer possible in Europe; but *we do not know this for sure.* Why not make the experiment? Since our system functions in the United States and has led us to the highest standard of living in the world, why not see if it works in Europe, before we support there the democratic socialist forces that we reject at home. We are pragmatists, we learn by experience; we have been very successful with this method in the United States; we have made a good many mistakes, but through these very mistakes we have made great progress. Why not do the same in our European policy? It can do no harm if we make mistakes there too. If it turns out that a system of American free enterprise cannot be maintained there, we shall be able to support progressive democratic socialists later.

All this sounds quite plausible.

It must be insisted all the more strongly that such a policy in Europe can have the most frightful consequences, leading to the greatest dangers, not only for Europe but for the United States and the whole world.

The United States is a rich country. A rich country can afford experiments. A man who needs 100 for his own consumption but produces 150 can make experiments in which 40 to 50 are squandered, and he will still have 100, which is sufficient. Thus our own experiments have caused no lasting harm.

But when a man is poor and instead of the 100 he needs he has only 70, or barely enough to avert starvation, then if he experiments, the 70 can easily drop to 50, *and that means death.*

This is the condition of Europe today, economically

and politically. Europe cannot afford experiments either economically or politically.

Let us assume that reactionaries take power in the countries of western Europe with American support, but that the crisis continues and they cannot remain in power, because the historical trend and the majority of the population are against them—then there is an overwhelming danger that *the Communists will come to power after the reactionaries.*

And then it will no longer be possible to change our policy and support the democratic socialists, as developments in eastern Europe have only too clearly shown.

The situation in Europe is too grave, the antagonisms are too sharp, to permit of such experiments as are possible in America without serious danger.

Therefore any direct or indirect aid to European reaction, which under present conditions cannot maintain itself in power for any length of time, is detrimental to the progressive, democratic socialist elements, and will drive large sections of the population to the Communists. Such support of reaction may *temporarily* stop the Communist puppets and the Russians, but in the long run it creates conditions favorable to them.

These are the chief dangers inherent in our policy. This is the time to point them out now that the

Marshall Plan is just beginning to operate and our policy has not yet fully crystallized.

If as a result of our present support of European reaction the Russians and the Communist puppets take power in additional countries, if they advance their frontiers and clashes occur on these frontiers, it is more than likely that this will be the beginning of a *Third World War*.

CHAPTER FOUR

EVEN A VICTORIOUS WAR WOULD BE NO SOLUTION. AMERICA WOULD BE AN ISLAND IN A SEA OF BARBARISM

THE CHIEF threat to world peace today is that some new Russian aggression in Europe or Asia may provoke a clash between the two world powers, the United States and the Soviet Union.

For the *moment* the danger seems averted. At the moment the wave of Russian expansion has to some extent been stopped.

But let us suppose that our policy of supporting reactionary elements in Europe leads to a fiasco, that the Communists and Russian satellites achieve further successes at crucial points. Will the United States look calmly on as the dike we have tried to maintain in Europe against the Communist wave begins to break; as Germany and western Europe begin to fall into the hands of the Communists and Russians; as the world balance of power shifts in favor of the Russians? I do not think so.

There are indications that further Russian expansion in Europe would destroy all remaining opposition in the United States to war with the Soviet Union; that if new Russian aggression proves successful at decisive points, the United States will answer with war.

WHY WAR WITH RUSSIA?

The arguments in favor of war would presumably be as follows:

Even today we are no longer at peace; we are simply in a state of truce. This is not a situation that can be maintained forever. A truce is justified if it leads to peace. But we see that this truce does not stabilize the world situation in any way; on the contrary, the situation is becoming increasingly uncertain and unstable.

Or a truce can serve a purpose—even though for the time being it does not help to stabilize the political situation—if for the duration of this truce the strength of the two contending groups remains approximately equal. Then, in view of the frightful devastation that would be inevitable in case of war, we should have to prefer a truce to a war, since it gives us time in which, it is to be hoped, the situation may improve.

But the relative strength of the two world powers—it is argued—does not remain unchanged; a distinct

72

shift is taking place in favor of the Soviet Union, **not** only in one but in many fields:

1. In the purely military field. Today we still have a complete monopoly on the production of atomic weapons. The longer the truce goes on, the more probable it becomes that the Russians will also begin to manufacture atomic weapons. This will not end our military superiority, but it will, of course, reduce it.

2. We enjoy immense industrial and hence military superiority. This was true even before the war, and we demonstrated it in the war by a military production many times greater than that of the Soviet Union; greater, in fact, than that of Russia and Germany together. At present our industrial superiority is based not only on our own industrial growth during the war, but also on the great losses suffered by Russian industry as a whole during the war.

Before the war the Russians had accumulated large supplies of food as well as arms. "These accumulations were insurance against the need which actually arose in the early years of the war," writes an expert in Russian affairs.*

The war has used up all these supplies. "Soviet reserves of food, raw materials, and other necessities were severly depleted during the war. . . . As a result, the USSR is now engaged in rebuilding its reserves as

* Harry Schwartz, *Russia's Postwar Economy* (Syracuse University Press, 1947), p. 8.

rapidly as possible and has established special ministries to supervise their accumulation for the needs of both war and peace. Until these reserves are rebuilt, however, their lack is a source of weakness." *

But already the Russians have begun their work of reconstruction and are carrying it forward with the utmost speed. In this they have been aided by an unusually large harvest in 1947. Every additional year of truce will help the Russians to surpass their peacetime levels of production. Before long, Russian stocks of food, raw materials, and arms may be expected to exceed peacetime levels. True, the United States will preserve its superiority, but that superiority may diminish.

Furthermore, the Russians have already drawn vast territories into their orbit: the countries between the Soviet Union and Germany, the eastern part of Germany itself. These territories taken together will soon be able to produce as much as the Soviet Union. And in these countries the Russians are the masters.

Today they are just at the *beginning* of this process of economic and political expansion. Strong economic and political resistance still remains to be overcome. But every further year of truce is a year in which all these Russian satellites will be more firmly co-ordinated with the Russian economy. In any future comparison of Russian and American strength, it is not

* *Ibid.*, p. 112.

74

Russia alone, but Russia plus her satellites, that will have to be considered.

3. The United States today is at the height of its prosperity. Income and employment figures have reached record heights. But will this prosperity last?

My book *The Coming Crisis** shows by a systematic analysis why this record prosperity cannot be expected to continue; why we must reckon with a depression, or crisis.

The *danger* of such a development has been officially recognized. In an address to the nation, calling for a special session of Congress, President Truman has declared:

"Millions of families of low or moderate income are already victims of inflation. These families are using up savings, they are mortgaging their future by going into debt. They are doing without things they should have.

"I know the worries of the breadwinner whose earnings cannot keep up with the high cost of living. I know of the difficulties of the housewife who tries to stretch the family income to pay for groceries and clothes and rent. I know how hard it is to skimp and save, and do without.

"When so many people are not sharing fairly in prosperity, the road is being paved for a recession or a depression."

* The John Day Company, New York, 1947.

Today, of course, it cannot be predicted *exactly when* a recession or depression will come. It is impossible to say exactly when, because our military expenditures, our foreign policy, our economic aid to foreign countries are such enormous factors in determining the outbreak of a crisis.

But one thing is clear and certain: If in this period of truce the record prosperity of the United States ceases, if a depression occurs with all its direct and indirect consequences, and if the Soviet Union is not affected by this depression, this too will change the balance of power in favor of Russia.

4. If in addition to all this the world situation changes in a sense unfavorable to us and favorable to the Soviet Union; if Russian expansion, after a period of stalemate, resumes again on a political plane; if the reactionary regimes we have been supporting collapse and are replaced by Russian satellites and puppets, there is a danger that the voices for war in the United States will predominate. People will say: To hell with this truce that is getting us nowhere. This truce isn't making us stronger. At best we are standing still, and in case of a depression we shall be weaker. Meanwhile the Russians are gaining by this truce. They are gaining from a military standpoint, because they are coming closer and closer to producing their own atom bombs. They are gaining in an industrial as well as a military sense, because they are accumu-

lating supplies, because they will soon exceed their peacetime level of production, because they are rapidly drawing the production of their satellites into their own economy.

If then the dike we have erected against them in certain countries collapses, and if we believe that war is inevitable in the long run, why should we wait for conditions to become even more unfavorable to us? Why not start the war today, under relatively good conditions? Why wait for the Russians to extend their territory still farther? Why wait for them to produce atom bombs with which to attack American cities? Why wait, when we know that the United States with its large cities and great industrial concentrations would be particularly vulnerable to atomic attack?

"The technique of war has brought the United States, its homes and factories into the front line of world conflict. They escaped destructive bombardment in the Second World War. They would not in a Third. . . . With the continued development of weapons and techniques known to us, the cities of New York, Pittsburgh, Detroit, Chicago, or San Francisco may be subject to annihilation from other continents in a matter of hours." * This was not written by any propagandist or journalist. It was written by

* The Winning of the War in Europe and the Pacific, Biennial Report of the Chief of Staff of the U.S. Army, July 1, 1943, to June 30, 1945, to the Secretary of War, pp. 1 and 118.

George C. Marshall, our Secretary of State, when he was Army chief of staff.

But all this becomes true only if the Russians are producing atomic weapons; it is not necessarily the case *today*. So why wait—if the dangers are steadily increasing!

Atomic weapons, it will be argued, are assuredly frightful weapons. But perhaps their use will bring peace. We dropped two atom bombs on Japan—and Japan sued for peace.

Russia is larger, Russia extends over two continents; and so we shall not need two atom bombs, but perhaps two thousand.

That is indeed terrible, and perhaps ten million or more Russians will be killed. But that is the only way —it *will* be argued, and is argued today by some people—to stop Russian expansion and aggression once and for all.

After our victory, there will remain only one world power, the United States. The war will not damage our home country. Consequently we shall be in a position to rebuild the world afterward.

Even today this argument, or variations of it, is heard in some quarters. The trend will increase tenfold if we suffer political defeats and the Russians meet with new success in their policy of expansion.

The argument that any new Russian aggression should be countered with extreme measures, even war, is tempting as long as we enjoy a monopoly on atomic weapons and are not ourselves endangered.

It is so dangerous just because it seems at first sight so realistic.

In reality it is based on fundamental fallacies. We must recognize these fallacies before it is too late, before we hurl the whole world, including ourselves, into the abyss.

HOW GREAT IS AMERICA'S MILITARY SUPERIORITY?

It is true that today the United States is far superior to the Soviet Union in military strength. How great is this military superiority?

The answer to this question, so critical for our future, is provided by an analysis that makes no attempt to minimize those factors that are not in our favor.

First of all: It is true, then, that the United States is far superior to Russia in military power. This superiority may be largely summed up in three points:

1. Our industrial production is many times that of the Russians.
2. For the present we still possess a monopoly on the production of atomic weapons.
3. We have the largest navy in the world and air bases not far distant from the Russian frontiers.

Let us analyze each of these factors.

Point 1: The industrial strength of the two countries. The Soviet Union has concentrated on repairing the enormous devastation brought about by the war. In large parts of European Russia this process is not yet completed. In those European provinces that were not touched by the war, however, and in the Asiatic provinces, production has already reached peacetime levels. Experts on the postwar development of Russia have come to the conclusion that ". . . by the latter half of 1947 the Soviet Union had probably reached a rate of industrial production approximating if not exceeding the prewar level." *

Then, when we take into account the 50-per-cent increase in our own production during the Second World War, the relation is approximately four and a half to one in our favor. (See page 43.) This, however, applies only if the Soviet Union stands alone; but all the countries between herself and Germany are her satellites, and in case of war she would draw their production into her own economy. Hence it is no exaggeration when the expert quoted above writes: "It must be concluded that two years after the end of World War II the USSR is in many respects far more powerful economically than it was at the time it was attacked by Germany, six years earlier." †

All in all, it can be said that the United States is at present about four times as strong as the Soviet

* Schwartz, *op. cit.*, p. 108.
† *Ibid*, pp. 109-10.

Union supported by the economic potential of the powers that it is in a position to control at the very outbreak of a war.

INDUSTRIAL STRENGTH DOES NOT IN ITSELF MEAN MILITARY STRENGTH

There is no doubt that four to one is an enormous superiority. However, merely to compare the industrial production of the two world powers is not enough. Such a mechanical judgment fails to take two important factors into consideration:

1. Industrial production is not in itself identical with military strength. The Second World War again demonstrated the truth of the military axiom that the victorious power must be stronger on the given battlefield and not elsewhere. An offensive war against the Soviet Union would have to be won on Soviet territory, many thousands of miles from American bases. For this a supply organization would have to be built up that would use incomparably more material and man power than the analogous organization built during the Second World War. This would mean that only a fraction of the total military strength of the United States could be sent into action on the actual battlefield. For this reason, if for no other, the true relation of strength between the United States and the Soviet Union is not four to one.

2. The United States has the highest standards of living for the masses of the people. This means that only a part of the total U.S. production could be used for actual war purposes. During the Second World War that part never amounted to more than 44 per cent of the whole.*

In the Soviet Union, on the other hand, living standards for the masses of the people are incomparably lower. The Russians will give military production a top priority. This occurred in the Second World War, and consequently American military production was not so far superior as a pure comparison of industrial output would lead one to suppose.

Although in 1944 the Germans were still on Russian soil and large parts of Russia were completely devastated, Russian military production in that year amounted to 35 per cent of American military production.†

And in a future war the situation will be no different. The actual military strength of Russia as compared to the United States will be much greater than the mere mechanical comparison of four to one in total industrial production would seem to suggest.

* Simon Kuznets, *National Production in Wartime* (New York: National Bureau of Economic Research, 1945), p. 124.

† Raymond W. Goldsmith, "The Power of Victory, Munitions Output in World War II," *Military Affairs*, Spring 1946, p. 71.

Point 2. At this point some people will impatiently declare: All these comparisons of industrial strength and military potential apply to the past. These things were important in the last war but would be meaningless in a possible future war. We have a monopoly on the production of atom bombs, consequently we can carry the war to the Soviet Union, while the Soviet Union cannot possibly carry it to the United States. This monopoly on atomic weapons creates an entirely new picture.

Is this true, and if so, to what extent is it true?

Many of those Americans who speak of atomic weapons today have in mind a push-button war, that is, a war in which atom bombs would be hurled across the ocean at Russia in pilotless planes. A war of this sort could be concluded in a very short time, without great loss in lives for the United States.

This is *a complete delusion and a very dangerous one*. We do have atomic weapons; but—as all American military authorities know and frankly state— there can be no push-button war for several years.

In his statement to the War Department subcommittee of the Senate Appropriations Committee, General of the Army Dwight D. Eisenhower declared: "We are all bombarded with premature conclusions about 'push-button' warfare. As Admiral Nimitz so aptly puts it, all we have thus far is the button. Even as the world still moves in terms of military power, so is military power still measured in terms of familiar, existing elements."

Concerning the reasons why push-button warfare cannot be expected for the next few years, Hanson W. Baldwin, military expert for the *New York Times*, writes:

Dr. Vannevar Bush pointed out again last week to a Congressional committee that the era of "push-button" war was far away.

His "debunking" but judicious conclusions are fully borne out by a nation-wide tour, just concluded by this writer, of the nation's principal proving grounds and development centers for missiles and jet planes. The new face of war is beginning to be seen dimly in the laboratories and test centers, but thousands of tremendous problems—some of them fundamental in nature—remain to be solved before the much-touted era of transpolar, transoceanic or intercontinental war becomes possible.

Mr. Baldwin comes to the following conclusion:

. . . It is safe to say . . . that no nation is yet ready for extensive missile war, for intercontinental air war or for transpolar war. No nation has combat models of transsonic or supersonic planes, no nation has yet been able to send a piloted plane above the point —63,000 feet—where human blood "boils," and no nation has a plane with combat range sufficient for

84

two-way bombing raids across the oceans or across the polar icecaps.*

In other words, if war comes soon, it will not be a "push-button" war. Quite some time will be needed before a transoceanic war will be technically possible; and all indications are that by then the Russians will be producing atomic bombs.

If war comes before that, true, we shall have the advantage of our monopoly on atomic weapons; but in a war against the Soviet Union, it will not be possible to use them any differently than we did in the war against Japan.

And this is possible in so far as we are today far superior in naval power.

Point 3. The United States has the largest navy in the world, while for easily understandable reasons the navy is the least developed branch of the Soviet armed forces. Consequently, our navy is in a position, without too much difficulty, to maintain communications between the American continent and armies operating many thousands of miles away. In addition we have, or can easily build, air bases from which atomic-bombing raids on the Soviet Union can be launched.

The overwhelming superiority of our navy enables us to operate against the Soviet Union from Asia as well as the Mediterranean and to organize atomic

* *New York Times*, June 29, 1947.

85

offensives against them from air bases, on both land and sea, at a time when the Russians still have no atom bombs and when push-button war has not yet reached the stage where it might conceivably be used against us.

WAR AGAINST THE SOVIET UNION WOULD NOT BE A LIGHTNING WAR

So far our analysis seems to support certain optimistic views. It seems to indicate that, if war with the Soviet Union should come within the next few years, a lightning war, if not a push-button war, may reasonably be expected.

But this is not the case. *It is impossible to defeat the Soviet Union by a lightning war*. The chief reason for this is the strategic position of the Soviet Union on the Eurasian continent.

We have repeatedly stated that the chief danger today is not that the U.S. will try to impose its system on the Russians, or that the Russians will try to impose theirs on the United States. The greatest danger centers around the political and economic future of the 1,500,000,000 people in Europe and Asia, who are living between the United States and the Soviet Union.

What is true politically is also true from a military standpoint.

86

If the United States and the Soviet Union were alone in the world, it might still be supposed that, in view of the overwhelming American superiority in industry, in atomic weapons and naval power, a war against the Soviet Union might be won relatively quickly by gigantic attacks on Russian cities and industrial centers.

But the United States and the Soviet Union are not alone in the world. The 1,500,000,000 people in Europe and Asia must be taken into account.

And the very fact of their existence changes the military picture completely, because *a war against the Soviet Union would have to be won not only on Soviet territory but in Europe and Asia as well.*

In order to convince ourselves that this is true, we need only ask: What would be the Russian answer to the threat of an atomic attack?

It is self-evident that the Russians are working feverishly toward producing atomic weapons of their own.

DEFENSIVE MEASURES OF THE RUSSIANS IN CASE OF WAR

But what will they do in the meantime, before they themselves have atomic weapons, before they can answer atomic war with atomic war?

In the present interim period the Russians are preparing a twofold answer to possible atomic attacks: (1) defensive and (2) offensive.

At present there is no completely effective defense against atomic weapons, and it seems likely that there will be none for the next few years. But for a country like the Soviet Union, extending over two continents, there are great possibilities of lessening the effects of an atomic offensive directed against it.

The Russians are attempting to do this in three ways.

1. They are increasing their military strength at top speed. In the early Five-Year Plans, chief emphasis was given to heavy industry. Although the Russian standard of living was exceedingly low, the consumers'-goods industries were even then very much neglected.

After Hitler's seizure of power, Germany greatly increased her war production. Of all the European nations, only the Russians answered this threat of war with a heavy increase in armaments.

Military Affairs * gives us the following figures on military expenditures in Germany (converted into dollars): 1935–39, 12,000,000,000; 1940, 6,000,-000,000; 1941, 6,000,000,000; in the Soviet Union, 1935–39, 8,000,000,000; 1940, 5,000,000,000; 1941, 8,500,000,000.

It can be seen that in the last years before the out-

* *Military Affairs*, Spring 1946, p. 75.

break of the Second World War, Russian expenditures for armaments were not much smaller than those of the Germans.

At the present time this trend is being intensified, in spite of the enormous destruction brought about by the war, in spite of the fact that the Russian masses today are far worse fed, housed, and clothed than before the war.

Every increase of production in Russia goes primarily into heavy industry, particularly the armaments industry. If the Russian masses are dissatisfied that after their tremendous sacrifices during the Second World War they should be compelled to live even worse than before, they—and particularly the returning Red Army men—are told by the Soviet propaganda machine ". . . that because Europe between the two World Wars concentrated on higher living standards Europe was defeated by the Soviet Union, which had prepared for war. They are assured that the Soviet Union must now prepare for the next one—the last great inevitable conflict against the forces of fascist capitalism—and that they must help." *

2. But what good does it do the Russians to increase their war potential in this way, if their cities and industrial centers can be destroyed with atom bombs?

The Russians are working to lessen the effects of

* John MacCormac, article in the *New York Times*, August 4, 1947.

atomic attacks by *the greatest possible decentralization of their industry*. For this the Russians are, of course, in an incomparably better position than any great European industrial state. England, France, Germany, all cover a very small area; consequently they are extremely vulnerable to concentrated air attacks.

The situation of the Soviet Union is quite different. It covers a sixth of the earth's land surface, and—in the present discussion this is extremely important—its industries are no longer concentrated in one region.

"During the four war years, industrial output increased 3.6 times in the Urals, 2.8 times in Siberia," * writes Harry Schwartz. The present, fourth Five-Year Plan intensifies all tendencies in this direction, distinctly stressing the Asiatic areas of the Soviet Union.

A most significant feature of this postwar investment program is the fact that more than half this new capital, 55 percent, is scheduled to be invested in the eastern areas never occupied by the Germans. Forty percent will go to the area from Moscow to the Urals plus Central Asia and 15 percent will go to Siberia and the Far East. The devastated areas in the west are to receive 45 percent of the planned central capital investment during 1946–1950. This would seem to mean that greater stress is being placed upon further expansion of the greatly increased eastern economic

* Schwartz, *op. cit.*, p. 10.

strength of the USSR, than upon rehabilitation of the once leading industrial territory of the Soviet Union.*

What will be the effect of this decentralization of Russian industry, this distribution of factories over such an immense territory? The effect will be, of course, to lessen the destructive effect of atomic attacks. More attacks and more bombs will be needed than if, as in England, France, or Germany, the industries and cities were concentrated in a relatively small area.

RUSSIA'S ARMAMENTS INDUSTRY IS BEING MOVED UNDERGROUND

3. The Russians are attempting to diminish the effectiveness of an atomic offensive in a third way: by building their most important munitions factories underground, with underground storage facilities.

In the Second World War, when the Americans and British started their continuous bombing of the war plants, the Germans answered by moving a considerable part of their war industries underground, by decentralizing production, by manufacturing parts in widely separated plants and assembling the finished product later. With this policy the Germans achieved incredible success, which, because of the false reports

* *Ibid.*, p. 21.

circulated here during the war, is still not generally known in this country.

In spite of all the Allied air raids on German factories and cities, German armaments production did not decline between 1941 and 1944; it did not mark time; the truth is that it increased by leaps and bounds.

According to an analysis published in *Military Affairs*, German armaments production, estimated at 20 for 1939, rose to 35 in 1940, remained at 35 during 1941, *but then rose in 1942 to 51, in 1943 to 80, and in 1944 to 100.* The article in *Military Affairs* comments: "When the invasion started and Germany was on the defensive on all fronts, her industries were turning out *three times as many combat munitions* [italics mine] as they had at the height of her military power in the fall of 1941, when the Third Reich controlled Europe from the Pyrenees to the Volga." *

This was the situation of the German armaments industries during the Second World War. Every one of us who is trying to form an opinion on the efficacy of atomic attacks on military objectives should know this. We should know that American and British air raids in the Second World War were not able to prevent *a tripling of German armaments production.*

There is no doubt whatever that the Russians are

* "Munitions Output in World War II," *Military Affairs,* Spring 1946, pp. 72, 74.

profiting from the experience of the Germans in the Second World War and doing everything possible to immunize their armaments plants and arsenals, not only to normal air raids, but to atomic raids as well.

The question of underground munitions plants, airplane factories, and chemical plants is no longer an academic one for the Russians. All indications are that work in this direction has already begun.

Of course, no publications are available on this subject. But what the Russians *are already doing* can easily be deduced from what the United States is *planning* to do in the near future. In this connection we shall quote from a report by Secretary of the Army Kenneth C. Royall:

. . . the concentration of industry is being studied, and a comprehensive survey of representative types of underground sites throughout the United States, including natural caverns and abandoned mines, has been completed, and the report distributed to interested agencies of the War and Navy Departments.

Since underground sites are an excellent means of passive defense, the War Department and the Army-Navy Munitions Board have considerable interest in this subject. In January, 1947, a Report on Existing Mines was prepared by the Chief of Engineers which presents factual data on mines in the United States which are potentially usable as underground sites.

The Chief of Engineers has submitted a proposal to develop construction and cost data incidental to moving a chemical processing plant (currently operating above ground) to an underground location where economic, geological and geographic features are best suited to this type of industry. He proposed further that a similar study and investigation be conducted with respect to an Ordnance Department fire-control instrument plant.

The Army Air Forces have been studying problems related to manufacturing critical aircraft components in underground installations. As a result of these studies it is planned to obtain funds during the Fiscal Year 1948 and direct the Chief of Engineers to construct a pilot plant underground for this purpose.

In the spring of 1947 the chairman of the Army and Navy Munitions Board visited certain parts of Europe to study the problems of underground sites and the dispersion of industry and also to study the general industrial mobilization plans of other nations. A War Department representative is following up these studies and is at the same time reviewing the current procurement and logistic systems of European nations.

With this in mind we can be very certain that the Russians, having for the present no atomic weapons, are doing their utmost to provide their armaments plants, arsenals, and food stocks with such protection against atomic war.

Moreover, there is no doubt that the Russians have worked out plans for evacuating the population from the most endangered zones. Obviously evacuation is easier in a country like the Soviet Union, where approximately two thirds of the population is still engaged in agriculture, than in other industrial states, where only 20 to 30 per cent are engaged in agriculture.

The Russian defensive measures we have analyzed are directed toward one great aim. This aim is that the political, industrial, and military apparatus should survive the first atomic attacks, that the population should not be seized with total panic, that the destruction of weapons, munitions, and supplies should not be such as to paralyze the Red Army.

But it is obvious that the Russians will not content themselves with defensive measures.

THE RUSSIAN OFFENSIVE IN EUROPE AND ASIA

It is certain that the Russian armies will survive the first atom bombs with negligible losses in personnel. Atom bombs are not weapons for use against dispersed soldiers.

Then, if in spite of atomic attacks the Red armies retain the major part of their armament, and armaments production is not seriously impaired, what will they do?

The answer is clear and unmistakable: *They will take the offensive, they will cross the Russian borders, they will occupy Europe and Asia.*

And if the war should break out in the relatively near future, it does not seem probable that any power on earth can stop them.

The Russians are the only great military power on the European continent. They were so strong that they could not be defeated by Hitler Germany at the height of its power, when the Germans mobilized the industrial potential, not only of Germany, but of all continental Europe against them. They could not be defeated, because even then their own military strength was not greatly inferior to that of Nazi Germany. Their own armaments production was decisive in the war against Germany, not the military aid that they received from America or England. Important as this aid was in certain categories, it did not, however, exceed "about one-tenth of her own munitions production." *

Today there are no German armies and there is no German armaments industry. If the Russian armies take the offensive, who can be expected to stop them from reaching the Atlantic? Certainly not France.

---

* "Munitions Output in World War II," *Military Affairs*, Spring 1946, p. 75. Munitions is used here in the broader sense: "Munitions for the purpose of these statistics include all aircraft, naval ships, guns, small arms, armored vehicles, ammunition, electronic and communication equipment; merchant vessels, unarmored motor vehicles, engineers' supplies, quartermaster items and medical supplies are excluded. This definition concentrates attention on the combat items that are of prime military importance." *Ibid.*, pp. 69-70.

Even long before the outbreak of the Second World War, French production had far been exceeded by the Russians. Both industrially and in military strength, Russia is many times more powerful than France. Moreover, the enormous strength of the Communist party in France makes it questionable whether the French army would function fully in a war with the Reds.

THE RUSSIAN MARCH TO THE ATLANTIC

There remain the United States, or, if England takes a hand, the Anglo-Saxon powers. But this means that if the United States is to start a war with an atomic attack, *large American armies would previously have to be sent to Europe.* (The American and British troops now stationed there are little more than a police force, adequate for maintaining order in an unarmed country, but by no means capable of stopping a Russian offensive.) It is an utter delusion to suppose that this can be done in the near future. At present we have no large American army; so far it has not been possible to convince Congress that military service is a necessity in this period of truce. We are not even in possession of all the weapons required by large modern armies. And years are needed for the complete equipment of armies that would have to fight thousands of miles away from home.*

No; if before starting an atomic war we do not have fully equipped American armies on the European continent, no power now in existence can be expected to stop the Russian armies that will immediately set out for the Atlantic.

Professor N. F. Mott of Bristol University, president of the recently formed Atomic Scientists' Association in England, stated rightly: "To call a spade a spade, the Red Army would not be stopped on its march to Calais."

That is the situation in Europe. In Asia it is no different. On the Asiatic continent there is no power with even the military strength of France. The only large tank and aircraft factories in Asia are in Manchuria; the greater part of them have already been evacuated by the Russians; and if production were to be resumed in some of them in the not too distant future, they would presumably be controlled by Russian puppets, the Chinese Communists. Even with all the military aid he has received from the United States, Chiang Kai-shek has so far been unable to defeat the

* In the Second World War it took even longer, but we have learned some things in the meantime. "We may, therefore, conclude that under present conditions in the absence of direct interference by the enemy it takes not more than 2 years to convert industry fully from peace to war production even if only few preparations are made in advance." *Military Affairs*, Spring 1946, pp. 78-9.

98

Chinese Communists. All China, the Communists and Chiang Kai-shek together, were unable to oppose serious resistance to the Japanese invasion of its cities and industrial territories. It therefore seems evident that if the Red armies move into Asia, they will meet with no major military resistance on the part of the Asiatics.

ATOMIC WAR AGAINST EUROPE AND ASIA

What then? What if the cities of Europe and Asia, the European industrial centers, are in Russian hands? What if the Red armies are on the Atlantic coast; if they have occupied Calais and Paris, Brussels and The Hague, Antwerp and Rotterdam? Then for the United States to win a war against Russia, it will not be enough to attack the Russian cities and industrial centers with atom bombs, because the Red armies, supported by an armaments industry that can keep going despite atomic bombing, will be in Europe and Asia.

Then the war against the Soviet Union would have to be won in Europe and Asia.

Then the United States would have to destroy the cities of Europe and Asia by atomic warfare, and in addition, drive the Red Army out of those continents.

Leading political and military authorities share our belief that the Russians, if threatened by an atomic attack, would advance into Europe and Asia; that the general staff of the Red Army has worked out complete plans for such an eventuality; that the Red armies are being trained for it; and that even now the Russian factories are working first and foremost for such a military operation.

In an article entitled "The Atomic Stalemate," Walter Lippmann wrote more than a year ago:

Russia is not Japan nor is it England, crowded islands peculiarly vulnerable to atomic bombardment. Russia has abundantly the only known means of defense against the atomic bomb, namely space in which to disperse its people.

Russia, moreover, has a formidable military answer to the atomic bomb. She has inexhaustible reserves of infantry all ready to be deployed into the center of Europe, and capable of overrunning the larger part of the continent. Against the Red Army in Europe, it would be impossible to use the atomic bomb without exterminating hundreds, perhaps thousands of Europeans for every Red soldier killed. Europe is, therefore, a hostage against a preventive war.*

Six months later, C. L. Sulzberger, in the *New York Times*, reported a lecture delivered in Moscow by Professor Eugene Tarle, the well-known Russian historian:

This is Professor Tarle's culminating point. He said:

* *New York Herald Tribune*, October 10, 1946.

"I shall cite comment from American military circles. The following argument was heard. War begins between the United States and the Soviet Union. The bombs are ready to pulverize Soviet Russia.

"What do the Russians do? Of course, they cross the Elbe and the borders of Manchuria and really proceed to occupy Europe. The more quickly a Western block is formed, the more rapidly will Russian seizures take place. Moreover, the Russians won't even have to fight. One out of every three men in France is a Communist, and France will accept the Russians without fighting. If there is any resistance, it is clear how it will end.

"What then? Bomb Leningrad and Moscow? Exactly nothing is accomplished. . . . There will be a war of nerves, but not only on Russian nerves but American nerves. Both sides will be unable to come to grips with each other!" *

The thoughts of Walter Lippmann and Professor Tarle were given additional emphasis by former United States Secretary of War Henry L. Stimson. In an article entitled "The Challenge to Americans," after attacking those ". . . who think they can make common cause with present-day Communism," he writes:

"An equal and opposite error is made by those who argue that Americans by strong-arm methods, perhaps even by a 'preventive war,' can and should rid the world of the Communist menace. I cannot believe that

* *New York Times*, April 8, 1947.

this view is widely held. For it is worse than nonsense; it results from a hopeless misunderstanding of *the geographical and military situation.*" * [Italics mine.]

It cannot be stressed too much that Mr. Stimson is opposed to a preventive war on *military* grounds.

If in spite of everything a war should come, there can be no doubt as to its outcome: We shall win. Our country, our cities and industrial centers, will not be bombed. Throughout the war we shall therefore be in a position to supply our army with everything it needs, while after a certain time it will be impossible for the Russians to supply the Red Army adequately, since our machinery of destruction will become more and more effective and, as the war goes on, our productive superiority will become increasingly pronounced.

THE PRICE OF AN AMERICAN VICTORY: BARBARISM IN EUROPE AND ASIA

Thus there is no doubt that the United States would ultimately win the war. But what would be the price of this victory?

The price would be out of all proportion to that paid by the United States in the Second World War. In the Second World War, England and France first opposed Nazi Germany; after the fall of France, Eng-

* *Foreign Affairs*, October 1947, p. 9.

land remained in the field; later she was joined by Russia. It was more than two years before we threw our full force into the war.

This time the United States would be in the war on the very first day and would have to bear the full burden of the war.

This time the United States, without any first-class allies, would have to reconquer Europe and Asia from the Red Army. It does not take a prophet to predict that the cost of such a war for the United States would be many times that of the Second World War.

In the First World War the United States lost approximately 50,000 men; in the Second World War we lost almost 300,000; in a Third World War our losses would run into millions.

But that is not all. It might be argued that these losses are inevitable, if the world is to be saved from domination by a totalitarian regime. But what kind of world shall we have after a victorious atomic war?

What will this world be like? It will be a world that has taken a long step, perhaps *the decisive step, toward barbarism in Europe, Asia, and possibly America as well.*

In the Second World War there was no atomic warfare in Europe. But today we know how close to ruin Europe was brought by the war. The social structure of Europe has been so gravely shaken that many years of peaceful effort will be needed to repair the damage

103

—if it can ever be repaired. And in the Second World War western Europe was a battlefield for only a relatively short time, while Europe as a whole, it must be repeated, was never the object of an atomic attack.

In a future war the atomic offensive would not be directed only at the Soviet Union; it would have to be extended over the whole of Europe. Atomic war against Europe, against its cities and industrial centers, would mean such destruction and devastation that Europe would no longer stand on the *threshold* of barbarism, *but right in the middle of barbarism*. And the actual expulsion of the Red armies from Europe would require an amount of destruction that would make the Second World War seem like child's play. And the same is true of Asia.

The price of an American victory over the Soviet Union would be: staggering losses, gigantic costs, barbarism in Europe and Asia.

One of the chief aims of war with the Soviet Union is allegedly to preserve the American economic and social system. Actually war with the Soviet Union, while saving the world from Russian totalitarianism, would hurl it into barbarism. It would destroy the foundations on which the United States has built its economic system and democratic institutions.

The Americans would be compelled to enforce "law and order" in a world of Hiroshimas in Europe and Asia. Everywhere outside of the United States the sternest despotism would be needed, even to make reconstruction possible.

The United States would no longer be a great state among other states. *The United States would then be an island in a sea of barbarism.*

It is a dangerous illusion to believe that it would be possible under such conditions to preserve democratic institutions in the United States.

No analysis of the purely military factors, no analysis proving the enormous superiority of the United States to the Soviet Union in industrial and military potential, should blind us to the facts. A war with the Soviet Union, though bound to end in victory for the United States, would be fraught with the most terrible consequences not only for the Soviet Union, whose cities and industrial centers would be pulverized by atomic warfare, but also for Europe and Asia, which would be turned into deserts. In a United States surrounded by a world of barbarism, all democratic and progressive institutions would be destroyed.

It seems to me that those who write about war and preventive war, though rightly fearful of further Russian expansion, think far too little of the dangers inherent in war today.

It is true that the world has lived through all sorts of wars, but a mere comparison of the Second and First World Wars should teach us that even in the last decades the destructiveness of war has increased many times. Atomic weapons represent another long step in this direction.

A Third World War, a war with atomic weapons, would not be followed by an American century, but by an age of barbarism, from which the United States would be no more able to isolate itself than it was able to isolate itself from the First and Second World Wars.

In his address to the American Legion Convention, General Eisenhower declared: "No great nation is today in a position deliberately to provoke a long and exhausting conflict with any hope of gain."

This is only too true. No great nation can gain anything by war today. Even if we win, we shall lose the exact same thing that we went to war to preserve: our free institutions.

If war against the Soviet Union is no way out, if it offers no solution, what then is the solution?

THE WAR AGAINST THE RUSSIANS MUST BE WON AS A POLITICAL WAR; THEN A SHOOTING WAR WILL NOT BE NECESSARY

Is there a way to stop Russian expansion and at the same time to preserve peace? That is the decisive question. It is the central question of this book.

It is the central question of our epoch.

There is a way.

106

There is a way to halt Russian conquest and aggression and preserve peace at the same time. There is a way that is also in keeping with the great American traditions: respect for the right of self-determination, respect for the sovereignty of other nations.

If we lose the political war in Europe, it should not be supposed that a shooting war will solve the problem. On the contrary: we must win the political war against the Russians in Europe and Asia; for if we win it, and *only* if we win it, will a shooting war become unnecessary.

CHAPTER FIVE

WE HAVE TO BE MORE PROGRESSIVE THAN THE RUSSIANS

IN ORDER to find out how to win the political war, we need only draw the inescapable conclusions from our analysis. We have said that world peace is threatened today because the mass of the world's population, the peoples of the Eurasian continent, *all* the peoples of Asia and Europe, are on the march; because the Russians are constantly trying to take advantage of this popular movement, because their continuous aggressions and expansion may unleash a new war, an atomic war.

We have also shown that by continuing to support reactionary forces we shall lose the political war against the Russians, and that our loss will be the Communists' gain.

A dike against the Russians and their satellites cannot be built by military measures alone. They have already broken through this dike at certain points in Asia, and they will continue to undermine it.

We must clearly realize that the Communists, though they unquestionably are a fifth column, are far more than a fifth column. They are the expression of the gigantic crisis in Asia and Europe for which countless millions are seeking a solution—thus far in vain.

NO APPEASEMENT POLICY

Does it follow that we can avoid war only by appeasement, by allowing the Russians to keep expanding at certain points, in the hope that they will abandon their aggressions someday?

I regard such an appeasement policy as a fatal mistake. Those who advocate such a policy have not taken into account the powerful forces in the Soviet Union that are driving the present political leaders to new expansion. It is true that the Russians are not *absolutely* forced to expand *continuously*. As their withdrawal from Iran shows, they can always put on the brakes, since, in contrast to Hitler, the Russian leaders have no great fear of losing prestige by an occasional retreat.

The Russian state will not collapse if it does not expand for a few years. It did not collapse when it failed to expand in the many years between the two world wars.

Yet, though expansion is not a *must*, powerful motives are at present driving the rulers of Russia in that direction. Today enormous sacrifices are still being demanded of the Russian masses. When Stalin exacted sacrifices in the period before Hitler's attack on the Soviet Union, he could say: We are menaced by the gigantic armament of Nazi Germany, we must not be defenseless, we must strengthen our military establishment at all costs. At that time Stalin was able to add: You are making great sacrifices for the building of the Socialist Fatherland, but even so you are living far better than the workers of Germany, who are doubly exploited by capitalism and Nazism.

The Russians were not defeated by Hitler Germany. They won the war; they won it amid tremendous sacrifices, and Stalin's policy proved justified in so far as the gigantic military preparations of the Russians were rewarded by victory.

But as a result of the war the Russian soldiers came into other countries, they came into eastern and central Europe. They saw with their own eyes that the German workers, for example, despite their double exploitation by capitalism and Nazism, lived a good deal better than the Russian workers in the "Socialist Fatherland." Stalin was no longer able to conceal this fact, for millions of soldiers had literally seen it, and they trusted their eyes more than propaganda.

Now millions of these soldiers have returned to the Russia whose cities and industrial centers were so devastated by the war. They have returned to a standard of living far lower even than that of the last years prior to the war.

If they thought that everything in Russia were subordinated to raising their standard of living through increased production, all this might still be bearable. But in Russia today a very considerable share of production is used for military ends, in an effort to reduce the gap between Russian military strength and that of the United States. This, of course, is a great drain on the Russian economy, since in comparison to the United States the productivity of labor in Russia is very low. The Russian standard of living remains worse than wretched, and little improvement can be expected for a long time to come. The leaders try to make the continued hardships acceptable to the masses by pointing to the war danger and the American production of atom bombs. This may suffice for a while. But not for very long. The rulers of Russia can no longer tell the masses that they are living better than the workers of central and western Europe. The soldiers have seen too much; they know better.

Immediately after the war, the Russians embarked on the political expansion that brought them into control of all the territories between Russia and Germany. As long as this expansion continued, it could be represented to the Russian masses as a great political success, although it brought no improvement in their living conditions.

111

For some time now this process of expansion has been at a standstill. But because the Russian masses expected something from the peace after their terrible sufferings and privations during the war; because with present emphasis on military production a significant improvement in the living standards of the masses is impossible; because millions of Russians have seen that not only the middle classes, but also the workers and peasants in central and eastern Europe live much better than they do—for all these reasons the Soviet regime is very eager to produce new successes and new conquests, in order to show its superiority over *all* other systems.

That is why the Russians, although they are not forced to expand in any particular instance, will continue to expand, especially where impressive successes can be expected, where territories important for the world balance of power are involved.

That is why any appeasement policy will fail.

The Russians will gladly agree to any compromise granting them new spheres of influence. But after they have incorporated these territories into their orbit, they will, in spite of all promises, undertake new aggressions whenever the situation seems promising.

An appeasement policy will not avoid war but will only postpone it—and during this postponement the power of the Russians will increase.

112

If military and financial support cannot by itself be successful, if appeasement must fail, what other possibility is there?

The other possibility is: *a basic change in American foreign policy*.

It cannot be the aim of American foreign policy to oppose the great process of transformation that is going on throughout Asia and Europe today. The aim of American foreign policy must be to work in harmony with this world-wide trend and so prevent the Russians from directing and *misusing* it.

We have undertaken to stop further Russian expansion. Good.

We have undertaken to erect walls against further Russian aggression. Good.

But we must learn that these walls will not be built in America but in Asia and Europe. We must realize that the terrain in those countries is not the same as in ours, and we must make a very thorough study of the terrain if we expect the walls to stand firm.

In the last analysis these walls will stand firm only if the countries and nations in which they are situated have helped to build them and are prepared to defend them.

But under what conditions will they help to build

113

them, under what conditions will they defend them?

The answer is: If they prefer us to the Russians; *if they feel that we are more progressive than the Russians.*

We are competing with the Russians, not in the United States or in Russia, but in Asia and in Europe; and above all on Russia's frontiers, in China and in Germany. It is here that we must be more progressive than the Russians.

WE HAVE TO BE MORE PROGRESSIVE THAN THE RUSSIANS IN CHINA

To be more progressive than the Russians means to bring the Chinese a higher standard of living, without depriving them of personal and political liberty as the Russians do.

To give China a higher standard of living today is possible only if we recognize that in China, as in all Asia, the struggle against feudalism can no longer be stopped; if we realize that no isolated reforms, but *thoroughgoing* agrarian reform, is needed; and if we are willing to help carry out such reform in those Chinese territories that are not in the hands of the Chinese Communists.

This requires a break with our present policy of supporting a corrupt government dominated by the

114

landlord cliques, without insisting on drastic agrarian and social reforms in return.

The *New York Herald Tribune*, which has done more than any other American newspaper to throw light on the reasons for our failures in China up to now, wrote as early as the summer of 1947:

The inefficiency and corruption could be cured only by the most drastic house cleaning in the government, particularly in the provinces, and by giving power to honest and able men who now hold some official positions without having much real authority. Winning popular support would be even more difficult. It would require action by Chiang Kai-shek and many of his subordinates based on the idea that the situation in China, as in most of Asia, *is a revolutionary situation and that devotion to the welfare of China's peasants could be a more important factor in the civil war than strategy or weapons or man power.* [Italics mine.] It would require a realization in Nanking that the great success of the Chinese Reds came only after they began to adjust their program to peasant desires. It would require an admission that the failures of the Kuomintang party, which controls the political machinery in China, increased in proportion to the increase in strength within the party of generals and landlords and reactionary politicians.

The United States cannot afford to back reaction in Nanking, no matter how grave a threat Communism may be, because reaction is so clearly doomed in China. In a smaller country it might be possible, as a temporary measure. But China is huge—the province of Szechuan alone has a larger population than France. *All the resources of the United States could not maintain in power a regime that was hated by more than 450,000,000 Chinese.** [Italics mine.]

Everything stated in this editorial has been confirmed, particularly that "the welfare of China's peasants is more important than strategy or weapons."

We can, of course, continue to send billions of dollars in military equipment to China and thereby keep Chiang Kai-shek's government in power for a time. But, as our experience since the end of the Second World War amply indicates, this military aid alone will accomplish nothing.

AGRARIAN REFORM FOR CHINA

What is needed is thoroughgoing agrarian reform. What is needed is that the poor Chinese peasants, the tenants and agricultural laborers living in territories now controlled by the Chiang Kai-shek government, should prefer life where they are to life in the Communist provinces.

In order to build a wall against the Communists and Russians in China, we must obtain the co-operation of hundreds of millions of Chinese. Only if the Chinese themselves build this wall will they be pre-

* *New York Herald Tribune,* July 23, 1947.

pared to defend it, because only then will it seem to them worth defending.

News reports are constantly reaching us of whole regiments deserting to the Communists from Chiang Kai-shek's armies. Small wonder!

China is a predominantly agrarian country, and nearly all the soldiers in Chiang Kai-shek's armies, as in those of the Communists, are poor peasants, tenants, and farm laborers. Why should these peasants fight with enthusiasm for their landlords, while on the other side their brother peasants, who have already cast off the yoke of their parasitic landlords, are fighting for the Communists?

That is why whole regiments of these peasants are deserting to the Communists—and they will continue to desert if they are not shown by *deeds* that a change has occurred, that from now on a government supported by the Americans means to do something for them.

That is why drastic agrarian reforms should be demanded of the Chiang Kai-shek government as a condition for any further American aid.

The objection may be raised here that this would be an encroachment on China's national sovereignty. That is unquestionably true; but military support of one side in the Chinese civil war represents equal interference in China's internal affairs, especially if

117

this military support is large enough to constitute the difference between victory and defeat.

The Russians and their satellites are everywhere making a mockery of national sovereignty. In China, Manchuria, Korea, they are supporting every move toward an agrarian revolution. They are effecting fundamental changes in the social structure of every country where they have any influence.

Our policy in Asia, in China, does not operate in a vacuum; it deals with *human beings,* with countless millions of poor peasants, tenants, and farm laborers, who judge our policy by what it does for them, compared to what the Communists are doing for the peasants in Red China.

All Asia, all China, is involved in this agrarian upheaval; our policy cannot ignore it. We must take a position. This is the crucial point. If we fail here, the Communists will be strengthened. Any purely military support of the corrupt Chiang Kai-shek government will at best slow down the Communist advance; it will not permanently stop it.

But if we insist that the Chinese government we are supporting carry out serious agrarian reforms, we shall have taken the important step toward *stopping Communist and Russian expansion in Asia.*

It will not be easy to make the Chinese government enact agrarian reforms—real and not paper reforms. So far we have had no success with the Chinese gov-

118

ernment in this respect. A correspondent of the *New York Herald Tribune* writes from Nanking:

"Some people here argue that to ask the present Chinese government to put through radical reforms is to ask it to fight a class war against itself. This argument is based on a contention that the regime depends on generals who want to run the army according to traditional, inappropriate and selfish politics, on rich people who will insist on evading taxes and conscription and on landlords who will always oppose land-reform projects." *

INDUSTRIALIZATION AND REFORM OF THE KUOMINTANG

As long as Chiang Kai-shek's government rests essentially on the old military and landowning cliques, a radical change is hardly to be expected. But this situation is not necessarily unalterable. We have already shown that *before* the Japanese invasion of China the Kuomintang also had a liberal wing consisting of the commercial and industrial middle classes and the intellectuals. It lost this wing after Japan had occupied the Chinese cities and ports. The United States has now liberated these cities and ports from Japanese oppression. It must now be the aim of American policy to strengthen this liberal wing of the

* Christopher Rand, "The Tragic Dilemma of China," *New York Herald Tribune*, July 23, 1947.

Kuomintang; and the United States is in a position to do this, since it can give economic aid in addition to military aid.

China was for many years a battlefield; its industry and commerce have been severely disrupted. China today is going through an agrarian revolution; *at the same time,* it must repair the ravages of the war and rebuild its cities and industrial centers.

The Russians can, it is true, support any Chinese movement for agrarian revolution, but since they need all their reserves for their own reconstruction, they cannot possibly help China to rebuild its cities and its economic life.

We can easily do this. Our policy should therefore be *simultaneously* directed toward the reconstruction and industrialization of China, and toward drastic agrarian reforms. If we help the Chinese to rebuild their cities and ports, to build up their industries, we shall be strengthening the liberal wing of the Kuomintang, which has always consisted of urban elements. If we help to provide a solid social base for these elements, we can attempt, by supporting this liberal wing of the Kuomintang, to win the government for the agrarian reform that is the central need of China today.

Only by going with the social trend in China can we help the government which we support to win the confidence of the 400 million Chinese. There are plenty of men in China who are ready and willing to carry

120

out the necessary reforms; the "third force" between the reactionaries and the Communists is of course not yet so strong as in Europe, but it does exist.

These men need our support in order to play the decisive role in China's transformation.

If we support agrarian reform and at the same time hasten the rebuilding of China's cities and ports by our industrial aid, we shall stop the Russians on the spot. Our military aid will then be only a secondary factor, since the majority of the Chinese people will be with us.

But if we ignore the agrarian transformation that is gripping China and all Asia, we shall continue to fail.

China is on the Russian frontier. Russian influence is already felt in a large part of China.

By insistence on agrarian reform, accompanied by aid toward industrialization, we would be more progressive than the Russians in Asia. This policy could stop the Russians at one of the world's most critical points.

WE HAVE TO BE MORE PROGRESSIVE THAN THE RUSSIANS IN EUROPE

Geographically, as well as politically and economically, Europe lies between the United States and the Soviet Union.

121

The goal of Russian policy—much as methods may vary in different stages and in different countries—is clear and unmistakable: to dominate all Europe in the same way that Russia already dominates the countries between Russia and Germany; to draw Europe into the Russian orbit—since Europe is of prime political and strategic importance—completely upsetting the world balance of power in Russia's favor. Of course, the Russians cannot conquer Europe at *one* stroke; consequently their policy is to impede European *unity* as much as possible; to exploit the antagonisms among the European countries, playing off one against another; to push forward at points weakened by national antagonisms and mounting social and economic difficulties.

The Russians have the advantage of being themselves a European power, and of being many times stronger than *any single one* of the other European powers at whose expense they are trying to expand.

FOR A UNITED, INDEPENDENT EUROPE

To be more progressive than the Russians, the United States must not seek to exploit the present difficulties of the European nations in order to draw them into our orbit. It must not attempt to impose economic and political forms that prevail in the United States but are rejected by the peoples of Eu-

122

rope. It must bear in mind that the European nations have their own economic and political mode of life, that they represent *a third force* between the United States and the Soviet Union.

The European nations must be carried through the present crisis, and they must be carried through it in a *progressive* way. The United States must do everything possible to minimize the antagonisms among the different European nations, since in this epoch of *world* powers these nations can in the long run hope to survive only if they represent a third force in their mode of life, and also are strong enough economically and politically to maintain themselves as an *independent* force in the presence of the world powers.

To work for a united and independent Europe, which will plan its reconstruction and industrial growth in a progressive, democratic way—*that is what it means for us to be more progressive than the Russians.*

EUROPE IN A BUNDLE OF CRISES

Europe today is not in *one* crisis, but in a bundle of crises, which are of course closely intertwined.

Three of these crises seem to me the most crucial.

1. Europe—unlike the United States—was a battlefield in the Second World War as in the First. It

is therefore suffering from the repercussions of this war much more severely than the United States.

2. In the twenty years between the two world wars there was never any real stability in Europe; there was no return of a prosperity embracing economic life *as a whole*. Political and social convulsions were constant. Even before the outbreak of the Second World War, the urban middle class was to a greater or lesser degree, in different countries, fast losing the very basis for its existence. This process was intensified by the war and its aftermath. In the United States the middle-class foundation for our system of free enterprise has hardly been impaired; in Europe such a foundation no longer exists.

3. Europe today must undergo a gigantic economic transformation in order to adapt itself to the changed world situation.

A COMPLETE TRANSFORMATION IS NEEDED

During the nineteenth century and up to the period of the First World War, the United States expanded from ocean to ocean; it had enough food for its population; it had the most important raw materials, coal and iron, oil and cotton. Consequently the United States became a great industrial country, in which foreign trade played a small role in comparison with total production.

Europe had developed along entirely different lines.

England, and later the countries of western Europe, had expanded far beyond their own borders. They had created great colonial empires. Europe had invested enormous amounts of capital outside its own territory; Europe became the world's banker.

The colonial empire provided Europe with raw materials and food. But not the colonial empires alone; in Europe itself the west was industrialized earlier and more intensively than the east, and consequently there was a very considerable foreign trade between the Europe represented today by the sixteen nations that have turned to America for aid and that other Europe which is now in the Russian orbit. This foreign trade consisted essentially in an exchange of the industrial products of western Europe for the raw materials and food of eastern Europe. How greatly the economy of these sixteen countries differs from that of the United States is shown by two figures, taken from the report of the sixteen nations:

Before the outbreak of the Second World War, the United States received 8.1 per cent of world imports; the sixteen nations, plus western Germany, received 49.9 per cent of world imports, although their production was not larger than that of the United States.

So great was their requirement of food and raw

materials. It is no smaller today if Europe is again to attain its old standard of living.

But radical changes throughout the world have created great difficulties for Europe's economic life. One of these is the gigantic transformation in Asia. The era of colonial imperialism, in which the European nations enjoyed such advantages in their empires, is drawing to an end.

The second change is that Europe has become poor in capital, that the whole of western Europe has become a debtor.

According to the report of the sixteen nations, western Europe was formerly able to pay for a quarter of its total imports with the interest on its foreign investments. Those days are over. Without American aid, it must from now on pay for its imports *entirely* by exports.

And third: The Russians are in Berlin and control the countries between Russia and Germany. To what extent Europe can hope to exchange its industrial products for the raw materials and foodstuffs of the east, even after the ravages of the war have been repaired in eastern Europe, is no longer a purely economic question, but a political one as well.

If Europe is strong, if it presents no weak points that invite and facilitate Russian aggression, *this trade will, by and large, be determined by economic factors,* for economically both sides stand to gain.

126

But if Europe, or part of it, is weak, the Russians will try to make trade a basis for political deals. And it goes without saying that the Russians, with an empire of 300,000,000 people behind them, will be at an enormous advantage in dealing with any one European state.

THE EUROPEAN CRISIS WILL BE A LONG ONE

Europe, once the richest industrial region in the world, must today carry out a complete economic and social transformation and at the same time adapt itself to changed conditions in Asia, Russia, and eastern Europe. It must do this at a time when, in contrast to the United States, it is *totally without capital reserves;* at a time when its economy has suffered a staggering blow from the changes that have taken place in Asia and eastern Europe, with which it was bound by the strongest economic ties.

The present crisis in western Europe is no brief crisis that may be ended in 1948, but a *long-term* crisis that can be overcome only by the greatest exertions. And until it is overcome, the Russians will have constant opportunities to exploit the resulting economic difficulties and social conflicts for their own expansionist aims.

But it also follows clearly from our analysis that Europe cannot possibly return to its old conditions,

127

its old economic balance. The changes that have taken place on the whole Eurasian continent are so far-reaching that the old balance is no longer possible.

A UNITED EUROPE WOULD BE STRONGER THAN THE SOVIET UNION

Europe must seek new economic and political forms if it is to endure as an *independent* force.

A united Europe of the sixteen nations plus western Germany would be strong enough to maintain itself as an independent political body between the two world powers.

The report of the sixteen nations includes a program of production to be reached by 1951. It provides for: "An increase of coal output of 584,000,000 tons, i.e. 145,000,000 tons above the 1947 level (an increase of one-third) and 30,000,000 tons above the 1938 level."

It further provides for: "An increase of crude steel production by 80 per cent above 1947 to a level of 55,000,000, or 10,000,000 tons (20 per cent) above 1938."

The increase over 1938, it can be seen, is not so enormous; it is absolutely realistic if Europe receives the American aid necessary to carry it through the worst period of crisis.

Yet with a coal production of 584,000,000 tons

and with a steel production of 55,000,000 tons, western Europe, with western Germany, will be very much stronger than the Soviet Union at this same time. In 1951 it will be as strong as the Soviet Union hopes to be (see p. 45) in another fifteen years, or after three more Five-Year Plans.

A united Europe would, in other words, be economically so strong that it would not have to fear any further Russian aggression.

Therefore a progressive policy of the United States in Europe must be directed toward a united Europe.

To a certain extent this has been realized by American opinion. We have invited the sixteen nations to draw up a common plan, to pool their resources, to help themselves. We have declared that the Marshall Plan is to provide aid for Europe and not for individual countries; and it is to be hoped that we shall make further advances in this direction.

But this alone is by no means adequate, especially if at the same time we undertake measures that will divide the European nations at crucial points and intensify existing antagonisms. But that is just what we are doing by our German policy.

This policy is all-important for Europe, for peace, and hence for our own future. Moreover, this is the field in which the need for a complete change in American policy toward Europe can most clearly be demonstrated.

The Morgenthau Plan provided for a drastic de-industrialization of Germany, a radical lowering of its industrial level as a means of preventing any new German aggression.

Today the complete absurdity of this policy has become evident. Ever since the end of the war, Europe has been suffering from a severe crisis of underproduction. Germany is the key industrial power of Europe. Situated in the center of the continent, it has close economic ties with every country in Europe. To reduce its production artificially is to delay European reconstruction and prolong the European crisis.

Therefore, one of the central points of the Marshall Plan is a considerable increase in German production, which in a relatively short time is to attain the level of 1936. So far, so good. But will the restoration of German industry—particularly German coal and steel production—not again create a basis for a new German war potential, which German reactionaries may again use to threaten world peace? What should be done to make any such German national aggression impossible? That is the crux of the matter. Morgenthau thought he could deal with this threat in a purely *mechanical* way, by artificially holding down German heavy industry; but as experience has quite adequately shown, this is identical with a perpetuation

130

of the German *and* European crisis (and, moreover, the present economic desert offers the best possible field for Communist and Russian expansion). This mechanical solution was bound to fail. Morgenthau did not take social forces into account. He forgot that German heavy industry became a threat to the world only because it was built up by the Nazis in league with the reactionary militarists as a basis for military conquest.

But what are we doing, now that the Morgenthau Plan has proved impracticable? What are we doing, now that the rebuilding of German heavy industry has been recognized as indispensable to European recovery? What are we doing to meet the danger of a possible increase in German war potential? What action are we taking that, in contrast to the Morgenthau Plan, bears some relation to the social forces at work in Germany? Are we doing anything at all to weaken the German reactionaries?

We are doing the exact opposite, we are supporting and strengthening them. We have put the British plan for socialization of the Ruhr "on ice." We did this against the wishes of the Ruhr population, against the express desires of the democratic socialists in Germany.

A publication emanating from German Social Democratic circles takes a clear stand against General Clay and his directives with regard to socialization.

131

"The Socialist Party of Germany favors socialization," it states, "if only for reasons of social justice and political expedience. It is intolerable that the same people who made Hitler great should be allowed to remain in their positions of power. If this policy is followed, it will be impossible to prevent them from repeating their criminal assault on the German people and the peaceable world. . . ."

For who are the "private managers" who are now to direct coal-mining operations in the Ruhr? They are the German reactionaries, the groups who were closely allied with German militarism long before Hitler, who helped Hitler to power, who supported him and the National Socialist movement before and during the war.

Reconstruction in the Ruhr *with* these men means support of German reaction. To all Americans who love peace, it should serve as a warning that this American policy against socialization and for the old reactionary management has not been the smallest factor in giving the Communist party its present strength among the Ruhr miners.

The Morgenthau Plan has proved a total failure; it has intensified the crisis of Germany and Europe; to-day we must pay heavily to repair the damage it has already done. But the damage can be repaired.

The policy we are pursuing today can have much more catastrophic effects. It was these very reaction-

132

ary industrialists in the Ruhr who have always been undemocratic, who have opposed all progress, who have always been militaristic, who threw themselves into the arms of the Nazis long before the war.

To support them today is to obstruct progressive development in Germany at a most strategic point. Democracy in Germany today is bound up with democratic socialism. To support these reactionary groups is, in the present situation of Germany, to support semifascists.

With American help, of course, reactionaries can for a time be maintained in power in Germany, but just as in China, this can be only for a time. These reactionaries never had the majority of the German people behind them, and they haven't the majority of the German people behind them today. After the world economic crisis they needed the terrorist apparatus of the National Socialist state in order to remain in power. Today that apparatus has been smashed. To remain in power today, they consequently need foreign support. America can provide it of course, but the danger for Germany—and not only for Germany but for Europe and the world—is that the Communists will be the successors of a German reaction supported by the United States. And a Communist victory in Germany would be a long step toward war and world barbarism.

Germany must be rebuilt; Europe needs German

industry. But it must not be rebuilt under a leadership that has always been militaristic and antidemocratic.

In the long run, it is not possible to collaborate with the Chinese reactionaries in building a wall against the Communists and Russians, and the same is true of the German reactionaries. Such collaboration, after stopping the Communists for a time, will provide them with the social groundwork for a Russian-supported seizure of power.

In a progressive and democratic Germany, rebuilding its economy and opposing the reactionaries at every turn, the Communists would have no chance; but in a Germany where Nazis and old-style reactionaries control industry with American support, the Communists will have *all the chance in the world*.

And the consequences of our supporting reactionary German industrialists go far beyond the borders of Germany. They threaten, indeed, to frustrate any step toward a united progressive Europe.

Up until now the United States has been one of the four occupying powers in Germany, and since the Ruhr, the heart of German industry, was in the British zone, the United States has not until now been the leading occupying power. Now this has changed. The United States is now negotiating to pay the largest share of the occupation costs. This means that the United States will have the decisive say in the whole western zone of Germany. The whole responsibility therefore rests with us.

What good are recommendations that the European nations should work more closely together to overcome the crisis, when our support of the reactionaries in Germany's crucial industrial region creates violent antagonism between the leading countries of Europe?

Germany is the neighbor of France. Any progressive development in Europe requires, therefore, that the progressive, democratic, socialist elements in the two countries should come together. This, in view of French sufferings at the hands of the Nazi war machine, is no easy end to achieve; yet it is not impossible.

But what are the consequences of our policy of supporting the German reactionaries, the friends of militarism, the collaborators with Hitler?

FRENCH OPPOSITION

This policy of ours meets with the opposition of the entire French nation.

It is a tragic irony that the French nation, so divided internally as to be menaced by civil war, is united in only one point: in its opposition to this American policy of supporting reaction in Germany.

De Gaulle and his supporters are opposed to it, because as French nationalists they view any increase

135

in the German industrial level with suspicion. They, like the whole French people, have not yet forgotten what sufferings were inflicted upon them by the German armies with their war production based on the Ruhr.

The French middle classes and democratic socialists are opposed to it, because this policy of ours undermines their own position in France, just as it undermines the position of their friends the democratic socialists in Germany. They know that this policy stands in the way of any democratic socialist progress on the European continent.

The French Communists are opposed; they are opposed to any American policy in Europe. But this policy of ours in the Ruhr gives them a ground for propaganda to the effect that the United States, in league with Hitler's old collaborators, is trying to develop Germany as an industrial and military base for war against the Soviet Union.

Is it not obvious that a policy that antagonizes every political party in France is not a suitable instrument for building a united Europe?

Our policy of bringing back the old German management of the Ruhr industries was and still is contrary to the wishes of the Ruhr population and particularly the working class. It is contrary to the wishes of the whole French nation. Finally, it is in opposition to the present British government, since it obstructs one of that government's central policies.

This American policy strengthens the reactionary nationalists in Germany and weakens the democratic socialists. It strengthens the nationalists, semifascists, and fascists in France, and there too weakens the democratic socialists.

GERMAN NATIONALISTS MAY BECOME ALLIES OF THE SOVIET UNION

But this is not the only danger. If the development of democratic socialist forces is thwarted by our policy in Germany, if the battle then boils down to the nationalist, reactionary semifascists on the one side and the Communists on the other, there is a danger that these two opposing elements *may come to an understanding* and join forces. Such a development, it goes without saying, would be actively supported by the Russians. Collaboration between German nationalist reactionaries and the Russians is no novelty. The story runs from Bismarck to the general staff of the Reichswehr to the Stalin-Hitler pact to the training of German divisions in Russia under von Paulus, former commander of the German armies at Stalingrad.

This collaboration has not necessarily been abandoned; it can be resumed at any moment.

137

All past experience shows that the Russians are much more adept than the western democracies at playing on this nationalist instrument. Thus the support of nationalist reactionaries in Germany is not only an indirect help to the Russians; it can play directly into their hands.

AMERICAN POLICY IN GERMANY MUST BE CHANGED

The only force that can stop the Russians in Germany in the long run is both antinationalistic and anticommunistic; it is embodied in the democratic socialists.

In order to stop the Russians in Germany, which is in all probability the crucial point in the conflict, *a drastic change in our German policy is necessary.*

It is necessary to change our policy in the Ruhr. It is necessary to bring it into harmony with the policy formerly pursued by the British Labour government. And it is necessary to bring it into harmony with the will of the people of the Ruhr, particularly labor.

For a really progressive development in Germany and in Europe it is necessary to break the power of reaction, of nationalism, and of all the allies of German militarism and National Socialism.

Democratic socialist forces and *only* democratic socialist forces can be a real bulwark against the Russians in Germany.

A change in our German policy will not only
strengthen the democratic socialist elements in Germany; its consequences will not be limited to Germany, but will extend over the whole of Europe.

It will go far toward allaying the suspicions of
those European nations that fear that American assistance in this time of severe crisis may limit, if not
destroy, their sovereignty.

It is not enough to point out that no word about lim-
iting the sovereignty of European nations occurs in
our official documents or in the reports on the Marshall Plan. It is not a question of documents but of
actions.

We must prove by our actions in the Ruhr and in
all Germany that we are on the side of progressive
elements, even when their economic policy does not
accord with our own. Then and *only* then will we be
showing the world and the nations of Europe that we
recognize and respect the sovereignty of all other
nations.

Only by supporting those progressive elements in
Germany that struggled and are still struggling against
National Socialism and German militarism can we
reinforce the basis on which the democratic socialist
elements in France will fight the alliance between the

semifascists, reactionaries, and nationalists in and around the De Gaullist movement.

But only if the progressive, democratic moderates in France are strengthened in their fight against De Gaulle and the Communists will a united western Europe be possible.

After the United States and the Soviet Union, the third strongest power in the world today is England. Now that the era of colonial empires is drawing to an end, England and western Europe will be drawn more closely together than ever before. Consequently the democratic socialist forces in England are the natural exponents of a policy aimed at a united, progressive, democratic western Europe.

But by our support of the reactionaries in German industry, we are undermining the European policy of the Labour government, the aim of which is to create a third force based on progressive, democratic socialist elements in England and on the European continent.

We know now what it means to be more progressive than the Russians in Europe. It means to work toward a democratic socialist Germany in opposition to all reactionary nationalists and Nazis. And it means to work toward a democratic socialist Germany as an integral part of a democratic socialist Europe.

Only a united Europe can be strong enough to

maintain itself in the present epoch of world powers. In a democratic, progressive Europe, victorious against reaction, the Communist parties will become harmless little sects. The social and political basis for Russian aggression will have been eliminated.

We are competing with the Russians in Asia and Europe; but with the Chiang Kai-sheks and corrupt landlords as allies we cannot compete successfully in Asia. The Chinese Communists would win out.

The same is true in Europe. If we give the economic power back to the reactionaries who supported the German militarists and Nazis, the Communists will win out in Europe.

A UNITED, PROGRESSIVE, INDEPENDENT EUROPE IS THE BEST BASIS FOR STOPPING THE RUSSIANS WITHOUT WAR

We can win in Europe only by allying ourselves with the progressive, democratic socialist forces.

If we succeed in bringing about a decisive change in American foreign policy, it will greatly contribute —but only contribute, since the main work must of course be done by the European nations themselves— to developing Europe as a third independent force.

And this would have decisive consequences for the future of the entire world.

Then Russian expansion would be stopped at the

crucial point, and not temporarily but for as far as we can see into the future.

The European nations had and at the present moment still have a higher standard of living than the Russians and their satellites. If the present crisis is overcome by democratic socialist planning, if the old standard of living is attained and exceeded, if this is accomplished by democratic means, without loss of personal or political freedom, then Russian expansion will have been stopped, for the Russians have nothing to offer such a Europe. This new Europe will be in a position to compete with the Russians in eastern Germany and among the satellite nations.

Above all: *Such a Europe would constitute a long step toward lasting peace.*

Russia, we have seen, is far behind the United States alone in military strength; but if a strong, independent third force is created in Europe, the military strength of Russia will be so inferior to that of the United States plus Europe that Russian aggression would become unthinkable.

A democratic Europe would be vitally interested in the preservation of peace, for only through peace can it achieve recovery and a new, unprecedented prosperity.

A strong, democratic Europe would not only be a guarantee of peace for a long time to come, but could

142

also exert a lasting influence on internal developments in the Soviet Union itself.

During the fifteen years after the October Revolution the Russians concentrated primarily on building up their own state and their own economy. Military expenditures were secondary. This changed fundamentally in the ensuing fifteen years of the Soviet dictatorship.

After 1933, when the National Socialists came to power in Germany, and to an even greater degree after 1935, when Hitler introduced military service and the danger of German aggression became increasingly evident, the Soviet Union itself began to develop a gigantic military establishment. The Russians went into the Second World War with an enormous armaments production, which had been built up years before. In this war their military and economic losses exceeded those of any other great power. Since the war they have been living in a state of truce, which now has been going on for almost three years.

Thus for the last fifteen years war production has dominated the Russian economy, and prevented any improvement of the living standard; it has also hampered any possible development of democratic tendencies in the Soviet Union.

Here Europe, as an independent third force, can exert an influence on the Soviet Union. First because the existence of such a Europe would greatly reduce

Russian possibilities of expansion and discourage military ventures; second, because such a Europe would somewhat attenuate the hysterical fear of foreign aggression that now prevails among the Russians.

That is why we must support such a Europe today, why we must help it overcome its crisis, and overcome it in a *progressive* way.

Today the alternatives are not isolationism and aid. Even before the two world wars, the United States was not able to isolate itself. Without our aid to Europe, the Communists would dominate the whole continent, and then the United States could not possibly isolate itself from the Third World War. The cost of such a war would be many times that of our present aid, and the United States would, moreover, be fighting under unfavorable conditions.

Nor is the question: Private enterprise or democratic socialism in Europe?

The social and economic basis for liberal free enterprise no longer exists.

The alternatives are, on the one hand, nationalism, fascism, and reaction; and on the other, planned socialism and democratic development. Since the fascists and reactionaries cannot maintain themselves in power—they were unable to do so in Germany and Italy, they cannot do so in Europe today—they would only be the precursors of the Communists. And Communist victory in Europe means war.

144

Anyone who is against war and for peace must therefore support the democratic socialists, must support a strong, progressive Europe.

Most Americans are not primarily concerned with the forms that European recovery and reconstruction will take; they are primarily interested *in peace and in avoiding an atomic war that can lead only to barbarism.*

Therefore, the American people should know the *real* alternatives.

The real alternatives are: peace and war.

In order to have peace we must stop the Russians; in order to have peace we must stop the Russians in Europe. But we must do so *with* the European peoples, not against them. We must stop the Russians by pursuing a policy that will give Europe a future as an independent, united force.

We must build a dike against the Russians in Europe. Let us build it in such a way that the peoples and nations of Europe will help to build it, *because it is theirs.* They will help if they can do so and preserve their independence; they will help if to do so accords with their own aspirations. And we must help them, even if their aspirations and hopes, even if their institutions are not and never will be the same as ours.

We should help them to live in peace, in order to save ourselves and our own institutions from the dangers of war that threaten to destroy them.

Let us help to build this progressive Europe.

If we succeed, then and only then shall we have won the political war against the Russians; then and only then shall we be more progressive than the Russians in Europe.

Then and only then can we stop the Russians without war.

DEMCO 38-297